D1256704

If You Had
Five Minutes
with the
PRESIDENT

5 Minutes,

55+ Personalities,

1 President

HarperEntertainment
An Imprint of HarperCollins*Publishers*

PATCHOGUE-MEDFORD LIBRARY

If You Had
Five Minutes
with the
PRESIDENT

Edited and with a Foreword by
RON REAGAN

IF YOU HAD FIVE MINUTES WITH THE PRESIDENT. Copyright © 2004 by The Creative Coalition. All rights reserved. Printed in the United States of America. No part of this book may be used or reproduced in any manner whatsoever without written permission except in the case of brief quotations embodied in critical articles and reviews. For information address HarperCollins Publishers Inc., 10 East 53rd Street, New York, NY 10022.

HarperCollins books may be purchased for educational, business, or sales promotional use. For information please write: Special Markets Department, HarperCollins Publishers Inc., 10 East 53rd Street, New York, NY 10022.

FIRST EDITION

Designed by Betty Lew

Printed on acid-free paper

Library of Congress Cataloging-in-Publication Data has been applied for.

ISBN 0-06-076069-9

04 05 06 07 08 ❖/HAD 10 9 8 7 6 5 4 3 2 1

*The First Amendment means
that government has no power
to restrict expression because of
its message, its ideas,
its subject matter,
or its content.*

—THURGOOD MARSHALL

Contents

Contents

Acknowledgments

As anyone who has ever written a book knows, it is never an easy task. So when 55+ people come together to contribute to a book, the magnitude of that task is all the greater. When those contributors have agents, managers, publicists, and assistants—well, suffice it to say we couldn't have done it without all their great help.

Our thanks to our longtime and committed board member Ron Reagan for bringing the final shape and sense to this collection, and for articulating so well what this book is about.

We also want to thank copresidents Joe Pantoliano and Tony Goldwyn for their leadership throughout this project, board chairman Michael Frankfurt for his inspiration, the entire staff of The Creative Coalition, which worked nonstop across time zones and the international date line to meet deadlines—Maureen Keren, Briana Haas, Charles Schrager, Shpresa Oruci, John Hook, and Geoff Rick served tirelessly. We thank Frankfurt Kurnit Klein & Selz and Helen Wan for their valuable legal services. And a special thanks to our "adjunct" staff—Neil Weiss, Jackie Hook, Ellen Arad, Jeff Vespa and WireImage, Marion Curtis and Star Pix, Kenneth Lexner, and Brian Zak—all of whom were called upon at all hours for all the odd jobs. We'd also like to say thanks to our "interns" Eliza, Danielle, Kiki, Jessica Hook, James Hook, James Adams, Andrew Adams, Alexander Oruci, and Jacqueline Oruci.

Michael Coffey came on board as editorial consultant; his eye, ear, and editing skills were invaluable in bringing these many voices to life. And Maureen O'Brien, executive editor at HarperEntertainment, with a brilliant mixture of patience and resolve, has made this book happen.

Proceeds from *If You Had Five Minutes with the President* benefit The Creative Coalition (www.TheCreative Coalition.org), the leading nonprofit, nonpartisan social and public advocacy organization of the arts and entertainment community. The Creative Coalition is dedicated to educating and mobilizing members on issues of social welfare and public policy. Headquartered in New York City, the Coalition also has offices in Washington, D.C., Los Angeles, and San Francisco. The Creative Coalition does not endorse or raise funds for political parties or candidates.

This project, an extension of everything we do at the Coalition, was a true team effort. We hope this book inspires and motivates you as it has us.

ROBIN BRONK
Executive Director
The Creative Coalition

Foreword
by **Ron Reagan**

© JUDY G. ROLFE/WWW.ROLFEPHOTOGRAPHY.COM

Well, what do you have to say? You've got five minutes.
Not five official minutes and then some hang time. Five
minutes. The president of the United States is waiting—
he's a busy guy; he's got a lot on his plate.

So there you are. All your solo rants in front of the TV,
all your drive-time jeremiads, the sputtering rages or spirited defenses, not to mention the near certainty that your
unique perspective, properly understood, will turn this
whole intractable mess around, have unexpectedly paid
off. You've got a shot at the title, a ticket to the ball. Now
that you've been ushered into the very heart of the White
House, this is your moment to seize.

You've settled into one of two couches arranged near
the fireplace of this peculiarly shaped room, at the opposite end from the president's desk. There are presidential
portraits on the walls. You're suddenly worried that you

won't be able to name the Founding Fathers. Sunk in the cushions, trying to regain some semblance of posture, you feel unusually short. The president gets his own arm-chair and looks taller than you thought. He seems to be scrutinizing you from nearly overhead. You can tell he's wondering why, exactly, someone has seen fit to carve five whole minutes out of his day for this peckerwood. Who are you? What's on your mind? The economy? War and peace? A factory closing in the Rust Belt? A hog-waste lagoon in Appalachia? Betraying just a hint of impatience—just a hint; he is a polite man and, despite the crushing burdens of world leadership, is striving heroically to be a gracious host—the president glances toward the gently curving Oval Office door. On the other side, peering through the spy hole, stands the president's chief of staff. He gives his wristwatch an ominous tap and nods to the president's secretary. A Secret Service agent leans into view. Inside, you find yourself wondering just what shade of white the White House is. Eggshell? Cream?

This is the daunting scenario The Creative Coalition presented to an array of smart, interested people from the worlds of entertainment and journalism and business—actors, comedians, writers, producers, etc.: You have five minutes with the president. What would you do with it?

Five minutes isn't much time in the real world—though it can seem like an eternity—but in terms of a presidential audience, it is, trust me, significant. Bona fide government officials plot, strategize, and wheedle for months in order to secure a little face time with the

POTUS. Think Richard Clarke. But crunch time is always daunting. Do you come on strong? Play it politely cool? You may think you have this down. How many years, after all, have most of us been giving a succession of presidents a piece of our minds through the TV screen or as we rustle through the morning paper? But actually being in the room is different. You can't throw a balled-up sock at the real president. You can, however, insult the vice president's wardrobe. I happened to be visiting on the day Senator Howard Baker took over as my father's chief of staff and was in the Oval Office when George H. W. Bush brought him in for his official welcome aboard. After shaking hands, we took our places in straight-backed chairs at the corners of the president's desk—I was to my father's left; Senator Baker and the vice president were to the right. I soon noticed Mr. Bush eyeing my jacket, a charcoal tweed with a large windowpane check (this was the eighties). Keep in mind that male fashion in Washington, D.C., then and now, revolves around the twin interlocking concepts of Brooks Brothers and the color gray. Clearly, my unwitting breach of etiquette had awakened the VP's inner frat boy. I watched as one corner of his mouth began to rise toward a grin. "Where'd ya get that sports coat—Hialeah?" he cracked, referring to a racetrack noteworthy as a tableau of WASPy sartorial excess. "Where'd you steal your suit?" I replied. "Off a dead banker?"

Generally speaking, though, a greater sense of decorum is maintained. This seems to apply to our contributors as well. Most have adopted a tone that, however strongly they may feel about a particular issue, is respectful and polite. Actor-director (and Creative Coalition co-president) Tony Goldwyn comes to mind with his earnest entreaty to forge a "sensible middle." So does Patty Duke. I had the good fortune to accompany Ms. Duke on one of the Coalition's forays to the Capitol to advocate for the arts and, having seen her in action, can attest to both her spirit and her decorousness. No surprise, her essay strikes a hopeful note. Some, as might be expected in such a diverse group, take a more pugnacious approach. Actor Matthew Modine seems to draw directly from professional experience, placing himself in the scene and in the moment and supplying dialogue of a sort—his own and the president's—to imagine a brief lesson about money and public policy. It's a verbal knuckle sandwich, and I'd bet even money that Matthew would leave the Oval Office in handcuffs, dangling between a couple of no-nonsense guys with extra-large necks.

Yes, it's a divergent group reflecting a variety of concerns and sailing off on various headings. Several have chosen a shotgun-blast approach, a laundry list of concerns—here are all the things that really piss me off; now get busy. Actor Peter Coyote tackles economic inequity, the environment, and public financing of elections. Actress-comedienne Janeane Garofalo manages to out-issue him, though, working in media consolidation, church-state issues, revamping the tax code, corporate tax fraud, public schools, and the Global Gag Rule, which denies funding to clinics worldwide that offer counseling about abortion. After all that, she still has the energy to go after prison privatization. Phew! That's a lot to chew on in five minutes. Other contributors—savvy advocates and veterans of congressional committee hearings—have learned to appreciate the value of editing one's presentation. Harry Shearer—actor, comedian, radio host, voice of Mr. Burns on *The Simpsons*—tackles campaign finance reform. *Saturday Night Live* alum Joe Piscopo weighs in on the state of our inner cities. The always acerbic Charles Grodin lashes out at sentencing guidelines and our burgeoning correctional system.

Of course, these essays tend to reveal their authors' personalities as much as they illuminate issues. Fans of actor Joe Pantoliano (the Coalition's other copresident) will recognize his mordant sense of humor, his aversion to taking himself too seriously. Young Hallie Eisenberg is a breath of sweet air as she laments the mistreatment of animals. Actor-activist Stephen Collins has some intriguing things to say about the power of meditation as a force for good in the world. And thinking-man's actor Ron Silver ruminates brilliantly on the virtues of internationalism. Then, uniquely, there is Harry Hamlin. Adopting the persona of an ancient shoeshine man, he travels from Grand Central to the White House—kit and all—to give the president a verbal dressing-down . . . and a spit shine!

I'm not charged with imagining my own five minutes with the president but, I confess, I can't resist. If we're talking about a generic President X, I would want to know his/her thoughts about Charles Darwin and his theory of evolution through natural selection (extra points given for familiarity with the concept of punctuated equilibrium). I know this may sound willfully arcane, but it speaks directly to the sophistication of one's worldview. Scientific illiteracy is troubling in those holding high office, as Margaret Carlson makes abundantly clear in her essay on the hypocrisy and general muddleheadedness surrounding our policy on stem-cell research. If you don't know where we came from, how can you determine where to lead? In the case of our current president, I would want to know whether he believes that the thousands of innocent Iraqis and Afghans who have died as a result of our military campaigns will be welcome in heaven (as he imagines it). People who believe they are acting with the mandate of God, who see others who don't share their beliefs as inferior in the eyes of God, make dangerous leaders. Just ask Osama bin Laden. How often does the president pray for the souls of these thousands? What would Jesus say about the necessity of killing children and babies in the name of a "noble cause"?

A word about partisanship: The Creative Coalition is a nonprofit, nonpartisan advocacy organization primarily concerned with supporting the arts in education and through funding to the National Endowment for the Arts. We frequently involve ourselves (I am a member of the board) in First Amendment issues. It comes with the territory. We presented our contributors with a generic version of our "five minutes with the next president" scenario—no particular president in mind. Perhaps inevitably, most have elected to address the current occupant of the Oval Office, George W. Bush. Had we performed this exercise five years ago, most writers would no doubt have found it easier to imagine themselves in the enveloping presence of William Jefferson Clinton. This is, of course, an election year, and an awfully contentious one at that. There is fighting in Iraq and Afghanistan and a divided citizenry at home. Passions run high. Many of our contributors take direct aim at President Bush. Others choose a more neutral path. But in no case was anyone coached, encouraged, or edited with an eye toward a particular ideological position. Nor did the Coalition make any assumptions about the opinions of the people we solicited. Potential contributors were contacted without regard for their political views; our only criterion was prominence in their respective fields. This volume reflects the thoughts and feelings of those individuals who responded and nothing else. As an organization concerned with issues of free speech, the Coalition is disinclined to take on the role of censor. Some people might complain that we are trying to advance a political agenda. Let them shout. The Creative Coalition will defend their right to do so till the last breath. Far from an ideological screed, this book is really just a snapshot, a thermometer dipped into a particular moment and unique slice of our American citizenry. Other times and different demographics would, of course, produce a very different collection. We make no great claims for this volume. It contains no grand thesis. One needn't read it front to back. Take it to the beach, to bed. Carry it along on the subway or on a long flight. Think of it as an offbeat companion—sometimes astute, sometimes merely irascible—whom one might welcome during the upcoming season of withering heat and politics. And while you're at it, imagine your own five minutes with the president.

May 15, 2004

Patty
Duke

Mr. President, I would like to give my wish list to you as an average Jane American. First, let me say that I cannot begin to imagine the horror of your job, the enormous responsibilities that must weigh upon you. But might I suggest that, to help you handle all this, you go deep inside your soul and forget everyone else around you and everyone else's opinion and find that place that allows that mistakes may have been made, that things can be corrected, that it is right to continue to fight for the right solution. If that fantasy of mine could become a reality for you, I think you would rank as one of the most brilliant leaders the United States has ever known. I believe we are in a wrong war and that there is an honorable way out. And after that is accomplished, think of the money that would be freed up to address other issues in this country—public education, the needs of the mentally ill and senior citizens. I ask you in particular to think of our seniors, who have seen it all, witnessed it all, worked so hard. They deserve all we can do for them. If the new drug prescription program needs amending, please have the courage to sponsor a revisiting of that bill. Despite these criticisms, which are really just suggestions, you are still the president of the United States, and I thank you for serving our country. I just want you to be brave enough to make it better. The job is never done.

PATTY DUKE, Academy Award–winning actress, past president of the Screen Actors Guild, and bestselling author, has worked for more than forty years in movies and television. Her Oscar-winning portrayal of Helen Keller in *The Miracle Worker* launched her as one of America's finest young talents. As a teenager, Duke went on to enjoy success in *The Patty Duke Show* before establishing herself as one of television's most versatile actresses.

Joe Pantoliano
(aka Joey Pants)

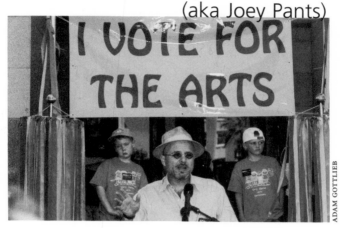

ADAM GOTTLIEB

So the first thing we do is we settle up this little difference between the Palestinians and the Israelis. It's all about land, but the present president and the president of Israel are not willing to give back the land that they took. My idea is to do with the Palestinians what we did with the Indians. We take their land and then give them a little land back and give them all casinos. Give them the *action*. I know, maybe their religion won't allow them to run the slots and the tables and play host to prizefights, but they'll get used to it. Fleece a few high rollers and you get a taste for it. In any event, that's not my problem. I'm just the idea man. The politics and all that the president'll have to deal with, whoever she is. What do they want for five minutes?

Now there's the North Korean problem to worry about. They're part of the axis of evil, right? Now, whatta they got? They got no oil, they got no value. All they got is the missile thing they're holding over our heads. But they also got, what, the fourth-largest standing army in the world? A lot of men on the ground. So my idea is, you cut a deal with this guy over there. You give 'em the money they want, but you make 'em be part of the coalition of the willing, you bring 'em in as the muscle. What, 400,000 troops over there, we put 'em in Iraq, we bring our boys and girls home. It's a win-win situation.

Right now Iran, the other member of the evil three, is not giving us any problems. They were a problem. But for now they're not a problem, so we leave them alone for the time being.

I think we can have world peace. You just have to give someone the option of looking good. A guy can look pretty sharp as a croupier; it ain't a bad living. And those North Koreans might like to get outta wherever they are just for a break. Oh, yeah, another thing: We gotta stop naming our missiles after Indians. These Tomahawk missiles. C'mon. Our ancestors steal their land, then we name these big missiles after one of their little weapons, a rock and a stick and a thong? It ain't right. We gotta upgrade the naming thing. I'd tell the president, she's gotta come up with something better. I can't think of everything.

JOE PANTOLIANO, actor, producer, and writer, serves as copresident of The Creative Coalition with Tony Goldwyn. His memoir, *Who's Sorry Now,* was a *New York Times* bestseller.

MICHAEL HIRSH

Mike Farrell

Dear Mr. President: I'm very concerned about the state of our country. You and I would probably agree that this is the richest, greatest, and most powerful nation in the history of the world, and that being the case, one might wonder what there is to be concerned about. My distress, if I may state it bluntly, arises from the fact that we suffer from a lack of principled leadership.

America's greatness, Mr. President, lies neither in its riches nor in its military power. It lies in the human potential understood by the founders and expressed in our fundamental documents. The failure of leadership is that over time politics has come to mean gaining and maintaining power for its own sake rather than, as Aristotle described it, the "taking care of the common good of all the people."

Once indoctrinated with the notion that we are the

proud possessors of "freedom," "liberty," and "equal justice under law," the people of this country have subsequently had demonstrated to them that these values are trophies that, once won, can be kept on a shelf to be periodically dusted and admired rather than living qualities that atrophy unless exercised.

It's not my intention here to make partisan charges or point accusatory fingers, Mr. President, but rather to express alarm that a nation founded on principles articulating the value and dignity of every being can have strayed so far off course as to put profit over people. It's no crime to make mistakes; that's an inevitable part of the human experience. But the unwillingness to recognize, admit, and rectify error bespeaks both weakness and arrogance.

The people of this nation, those who claim it by birthright and those who have responded to its beacon of hope, want to believe in what America stands for. They want this because it means they matter. There is no single thing more important, Mr. President, than the understanding that the people of this country—and by extension the people of the world—have lives that matter. That they do not now have this is evidenced daily by demonstrations of careless disregard for themselves and others, by wanton acts of cruelty, violence, and self-destruction. Drug use, child and spousal abuse, self-abuse, suicide, murder, and other forms of lawless and antisocial behavior are not signs of weakness or moral turpitude; they are manifestations of fear, confusion, hopelessness, and misdirected rage. They are the legacy of an absence of leadership.

Leadership, sir, is not imposing your will on the people; nor is it using the power of your office to impose your political will on those of other nations. Leadership is inspiring self-appreciation and exhorting into practice the spirit of America.

This can be done rather simply, given the position of power the American presidency has assumed. Some of it can be done by fiat, some by legislation, some by inspiration. First it requires a declaration that America is the hope of the world not because it is the richest and most powerful among nations, but because it embodies the aspirations of humankind on its journey from the caves to the stars. Second, it requires actions demonstrating that our national energies will henceforth be expended solely in pursuit of human enhancement.

For example:

Proclaim that discrimination or exploitation of any type on the basis of age, race, creed, color, gender, or sexual preference is contrary to American values and will not be tolerated.

Declare the preservation of our Earth and its natural resources an urgent priority and ban further exploitation or pollution of our oceans, wilderness areas, rivers, lakes, and skies.

Declare that our national security is far more than a military matter and shift spending priorities away from building redundant weapons systems and into rebuilding and refurbishing our nation's schools while returning music, arts, and culture to our educational curriculum. Government grants guaranteeing a college education to all interested students can be repaid by a two-year national service requirement that includes a nonmilitary option.

Declare that the priorities of this government will no longer tolerate homelessness and joblessness. A job-training program coupled with a project to build low-cost, affordable housing, expanding on the model of Habitats for Humanity, for example, will put jobless people to work on the needs of the homeless.

Devise a national health-care system that includes psychiatric care to ease the financial and emotional burden on Americans and begin to address the horror of having more mentally ill in our prisons than in our mental institutions.

Develop environmentally sound fuels and technologies that increase the opportunities for business to create profits without pollution. Programs to assist cities to develop and build pollution-free public transit systems will aid local economies, create jobs, and ease environmental damage.

Declare that a criminal justice system focused on rehabilitation and free of the taint of racism and classism is the only goal of a Justice Department worthy of the name.

These are but a few life-enhancing, nation-building, world-altering initiatives, Mr. President. They are a way to rekindle hope. What's lacking is the willingness to lead.

MIKE FARRELL is an actor, producer, writer, and director; the cochair of Human Rights Watch in Southern California; the president of the Board of Death Penalty Focus; the spokesperson for Concern America, an international refugee aid and relief organization; and a goodwill ambassador for the United Nations High Commissioner for Refugees. Television fans will remember him as B. J. Hunnicut on *M*A*S*H* and later as Dr. James Hansen on NBC's *Providence.*

ANTHONY MANDLER

Ron Silver

I want to talk to you about one issue, the issue that has predominated since 9/11, and that's the danger posed by twenty-first century terrorism, arising from the possibility that terrorist groups will access and use weapons of mass destruction. It is an existential question. Terrorist groups exist. Weapons of mass destruction exist.

What is the appropriate way for America to respond? What is the appropriate use of American military force in today's world? Indeed, what is the proper role for America in the twenty-first century?

Are we expected to use our unique capabilities to intervene in humanitarian crises (Cambodia, Rwanda, Bosnia, Kosovo, or Darfur) but refrain from using our military might to defend ourselves and what we perceive to be our national interests?

Do we believe in the use of force, as a last resort, to defend our values, Western values?

Are our values universally applicable?

It is popular in certain quarters to say that we have no right to impose democracy, pluralism, and tolerance on nations that have no such tradition. But can that be the case when that other tradition is bound and determined by any means to destroy ours?

Is peace preferable to war? Of course it is. Peace is always preferable to war. But I don't think that is the question we need to be asking. The question is: Peace at what price? Peace at what risk? Peace for how long? In 1937, for many people, there were very good reasons not to go to war with the fascists; strong, reasonable, sensible reasons. By 1945 those same people wished they had gone to war earlier. Mr. President, look at any of Charles Lindbergh's speeches at the many America First rallies in which he preached nonintervention in Europe.

Are people's fears exacerbated by the government or the media? On the contrary. I don't think we are afraid enough. Many people are in denial, and their rational, humane sensibilities look for rational, humane, and sensible answers. There is a misunderstanding about what's at stake. We *are* in a war, unlike any other since our nation was founded.

So what should we do, Mr. President?

What I would like to see is an extended national conversation about America's role in the world. Is it possible to arrive at a consensus, as we have in the past? Or are we condemned to a lot of posturing on both sides of the aisle that is ignorant, sometimes willfully so, of what has gone on before? When President Clinton avoided the UN and bombed and made war on Kosovo, was that appropriate or not? What was America's interest?

The world order we've gotten used to over the last half century is crumbling, and post-1945 institutions are anachronistic. The UN cannot be trusted to do the right thing if history is any guide. There were UN blue helmets on the ground in Srebrenica and Rwanda. It can barely bring itself to condemn the genocide in Darfur, Sudan.

But this is no surprise. At its inception, Stalin and Mao Tse-tung held two of the Security Council's five seats. Mr. President, it is time to reform that organization. The EU gets one seat, which they can rotate among its members. Perhaps Brazil, India certainly, gets a seat, along with Japan and an African country. Why not, Mr. President?

Mr. President, the only real threat America poses to the world is not projection of its influence but withdrawal from global crises.

Mr. President, along with Samuel Johnson we know that the fact of twilight does not mean there is no day or night. You, sir, can lead this nation into a conversation about choosing day or night. Recognition. Clarity. Determination. Patience.

RON SILVER was the founding president of The Creative Coalition.

Hallie
Eisenberg

KERRY LEA

Mr. President, as a twelve-year-old seventh grader, I am here today to ask that you support two things that I think are very important. Please support arts education in the schools all through elementary, middle, and high school. The arts offer a way to learn what books and lecturing can't teach alone. I've been fortunate to have experienced this many times. One example is when we were learning about Helen Keller at my school. Since I portrayed Helen Keller in a film version of *The Miracle Worker,* the teacher thought it would be interesting to learn about this amazing woman by putting on the play. I already knew how to communicate in sign language from doing the film, so I helped all the students in my class learn how to sign as well. And putting on the play in school helped us all learn far more about what it is like to be blind and deaf than we ever could have from a book. After the play, the students were eager to learn more about Helen Keller, and they began to feel that children with disabilities were not so different from them. It takes special teachers and a good space and resources for costumes and after-school supervision to do plays, but involvement in the arts provides incredibly worthwhile learning experiences. And I think the president could use his leadership to support such arts programs.

The other important issue to me is how animals are treated in slaughterhouses and factory farms. I have been a vegetarian for more than a year, and I am now a vegan, because I've learned how horribly animals are treated in some meatpacking companies and at some poultry farms, and I just can't bring myself to eat meat or animal products. I'm not against other people eating them, but if more people could see—like I did—how animals suffer at many factory farms, I imagine they would be moved to support anything we could do to make the treatment of those animals more humane. We saw recently what can happen, with mad cow disease, if the conditions are too harsh for the animals. It's bad for us as well as the animals. The federal government can enforce more humane standards in the meat and dairy industries. It might be hard to get everyone involved to agree to more safeguards and better conditions, but it would sure be worth the investment in the long run. After all, our safety and the animals' safety really go hand in hand. As a leadership country, we should be a role model for the rest of the world.

HALLIE EISENBERG is one of America's most successful child actors, with numerous roles on both stage and screen to her credit. She has starred in twelve movies, including *The Insider* and *Bicentennial Man*. Hallie is the youngest ever member of The Creative Coalition.

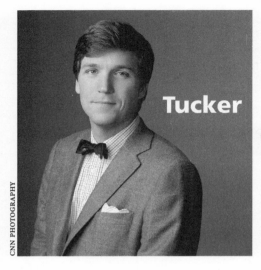

CNN PHOTOGRAPHY

Tucker Carlson

Congratulations, Mr. President-elect! The polls just closed an hour ago, so I can imagine that your head must still be spinning. I'm sure you're eager to finish washing your hands, leave the men's room, and head off to a much-deserved vacation. I don't want to keep you. But since you're here, and I'm blocking the door, here's some unsolicited advice about your new job:

Don't overreach. Let your rhetoric soar, but keep your goals modest. You're not going to change human nature over the next four years. You'll be lucky to shorten the line at the DMV. There's no shame in this. Forget just about everything you said during the campaign and admit the obvious: It's a pretty nice country already. At best, you'll be able to make minor improvements on the margins.

At worst, you could really screw it up. It's a lot easier to break things than it is to create them. Keep that in mind the next time you're tempted to tell other people how to live their lives. Human systems evolve for a reason. Tamper with them at your peril.

Sometimes, of course, you won't be able to resist. When you do attempt to change things, explain yourself. Tell us why you're doing it. Explaining, after all, is your job. Even the smartest presidents forget this. After a year or two in office, you may feel like king. You're not. You can't even make laws, only veto them. Instead, your role is to make your case, to the Congress and to the country. Your words are your currency. You're rhetorician-in-chief.

You'll often hear people claim they watch what a leader does, not what he says. This is a crock. Presidents are remembered for their words, for their ability to inspire and change the minds of the citizens they lead.

So speak. Do it often. Do it in plain language. Do it until the rest of us understand what you mean.

Finally, Mr. President-elect, remember what makes America great. No doubt you'll speak eloquently of our freedom and our democracy and of the basic decency of our citizens, and you should. These are marvelous things. But they're not the whole story. America is a great country for still another reason: We have terrific airports. You can catch a breakfast flight out of Washington and be on the other side of the continent in time for an early lunch. Just as easily you can fly home. You can do this every day of the week.

And not just you. Air travel in America is cheap and

safe, and accessible to everyone. It brings families together. It is an engine of our prosperity. It is also a metaphor for the people we are: ambitious, forward-looking, far-flung, and yet connected. There's a reason terrorists target airplanes. They are a symbol of what it is to be American.

Yet our airports could be better. We need many more of them, for one thing. Daily parking should be far closer to the terminal. And those bored-looking screeners in polyester uniforms who shuffle around all day impeding progress at the X-ray machines? Please. They're an embarrassment, not just to our nation, but to the very idea of human progress.

These are problems you realistically could do something about. A grateful nation would thank you if you did.

Good luck and Godspeed. Your third year in office will be horrible. They always are. Keep your sense of humor, try not to lie too much, and you'll likely be just fine.

TUCKER CARLSON is cohost of *Crossfire*, CNN's popular political debate program. He is also a political analyst for CNN. Formerly a staff writer at the *Arkansas Democrat-Gazette* in Little Rock, Carlson has been a columnist for *New York* magazine and *Reader's Digest*. He now writes for *Esquire*. Carlson's book *Politicians, Partisans, and Parasites: My Adventures in Cable News* was published in 2003.

Janeane Garofalo

KENT LANIER

Hey, thanks for your time. I know you must be busy. I like to think so, anyway. So here's my hit parade of hopes and dreams. . . .

Media consolidation and deregulation is a big problem—if there's an hour of right-wing commentary here's the hour of left-wing commentary, or my five minutes, anyway: the deregulation that occurred in 1996 under Clinton has to be reexamined and subjected to new regulations so there aren't so few owners across media markets. How about you swap your first state dinner for the First Annual End to Right-Wing Radio Talk Shows Barbecue! It'll be great. Big turnout, big laughs, hard whiskey—and no pork. Nah. On second thought, the White House shouldn't be sucking up to the media in any way! We have a hard enough time doing our job as it is. Try a few more press conferences, will ya?

I have a few items here to mention. When are you going to commit to a separation of church and state, especially now that we've been drawn into what the enemy is calling a "holy war," when we should really be fighting for democracy—the democracy founded on the right to religious freedom, remember?

While you're at it, can someone undo the Global Gag Rule? There is now such a rule, thanks to an executive order, which has the effect of endangering health care for women around the world because we disallow international support for organizations with reproductive rights and planned parenting on their agendas. A little short-sighted in a world that features way too much starvation. I know, there's the Christian right to worry about. But see above: church and state, separation of . . .

You're looking at your watch!

Revamp and refund the IRS to enable them to go after corporate criminals; let's get the corporate welfare out of the tax code, too.

And let's not forget the once crown jewel of our country—the public schools. Mr./Ms. President, I know education is a local issue, but isn't it about time that we made funding for the public schools a priority? Our current system, which depends primarily on property taxes, is an absurd caste system, making for a have and have-not society, with poorer communities being brought low by a poor tax base. It eats away at the heart of their hope—kids' education.

And do you know about the increasing privatization

of our prisons? It has really gotten out of hand. Someone's living high off that system. These companies are reaping exorbitant profits from taxpayer money. Do we really want our corrections to be handled by a private sector looking to fatten margins by getting a deal on toothpaste? The whole national prison system has to be—

What? You don't have to show me the door, I know what one looks like. Hey, yeah, thanks for your time. . . . You're really telling me to rest assured? Oh, I'm rested. Assured? Hardly.

JANEANE GAROFALO, stand-up comedienne and actress, received two Emmy nominations for her work on *The Larry Sanders Show.* In 1999 she and Ben Stiller wrote *Feel This Book: An Essential Guide to Self-Empowerment, Spiritual Supremacy, and Sexual Satisfaction.* Currently, Garofalo and Al Franken lend their voices, wit, and wisdom to Air America, the national liberal radio station that debuted in 2004.

Antwone Fisher

LEROY HAMILTON

Mr. President, it would be my wish that, among the mountain of things you have to do, you could give your heart and hand to the kids in this country who have no true home. Now, the American people surely have a large heart. But while more than twenty thousand children a year from abroad are adopted by American couples, here at home children orphaned or otherwise left without parenting can't find placement in the adoption system. For them, it is foster care, which is often an endlessly revolving door. I am one of them. I was a foster kid for eighteen years. As the kids get older, they have even less and less of a chance to find adoptive parents, parents who will be with them for a lifetime. I have nothing against people who adopt a kid from Asia or South America or wherever. They have good hearts, and bless them. But I just ask that they consider the idea that charity begins at home. Would you give the food you had to a neighbor's kids and let your own go hungry? I have talked to lots of people and I know they think they are being more charitable by adopting kids from overseas. They feel proud, and they should. And, in their defense, they may have found that going abroad involves less red tape than trying to adopt here in America. Mr. President, it would be a great service to our own children if you could empower a study of adoption at home, and how to make it more feasible.

If a natural parent can't step up to the plate, then we, as a country, before letting that kid enter a foster system, should encourage legal adoption. Maybe there could be tax incentives or school or health-care incentives to make it easier to adopt at home. People fight for lots of things in this country, and often win—abortion rights, gay and lesbian rights, animal rights. Why not the rights of unwanted or uncared-for kids right here, U.S. citizens?

Every time I mention this, it ruffles some feathers. Those who have done it—gone abroad and brought a little child back—give me a hard time, like I am charging them with some kind of crime. I'm not. I'm just asking that people look a little closer to home. When American couples stopped at a red light see that teenage boy jump up on the hood with his squeegee, that boy is me. That boy could have been in a nice car, on the other side of that windshield he's swabbing, except for a system that overlooked him, right here on our streets, and brought babies home from other parts of the world. That's a problem, it seems to me, and I would ask you, as president, to see what you can do about it.

ANTWONE FISHER works as a screenwriter, author, and film producer. His *New York Times* bestseller, *Finding Fish: A Memoir,* is the story of his life's journey. The film *Antwone Fisher* is based on his life and was written by Fisher.

Fisher Stevens

Dear Mr. President: The world is in a crucial and dangerous place right now, and there needs to be an epic shift in
the way people communicate and think. It has become a
world of righteousness and narrow-mindedness; it seems
there is a myopic point of view all over the world. We
need a shift in consciousness. We have to start thinking
that we and the world are all in this together. Right now,
the world is polarized, and much of the world is against
us. Are they against all that we think is right? Of course
not. So we must look more carefully, openly, at what it is
about American values or actions that is not finding support in parts of the world community.

I think the big problem, Mr. President, is that we no
longer know who we are as a nation. Our country is more
divided now than at any time since the Civil War. There
doesn't seem to be one kind of American. We need a pres-

ident who can understand this and not dictate who or what is an American. Our world is getting smaller and smaller and technology is now playing a larger role, bringing the world closer and closer at a staggering rate. But the increasing interrelatedness in the world can have devastating effects if not handled carefully.

Therefore, the president must understand the importance of building friendships abroad and not arrogantly going about telling other countries how to be. We need someone who can put himself in the other guy's shoes and have a deeper understanding of who he is. Also, Mr. President, in our Constitution it is written quite clearly that there should be a separation between church and state. Our president should not be leading us on a mission for his "god." The president's god is not necessarily my god, or the god of the rest of the American people.

Consider the environment, Mr. President. We have not joined the world community in a global effort to protect air and water and the problems of climate change. We could be leading the way, and should be. But we are not.

For our way of life to be convincing, we must start to clean up at home. We must make alliances here as part of our effort to form alliances abroad for a good that will benefit America and the world, which really should be viewed as one.

Lastly, let me ask you, as president, to admit mistakes when they are made. Don't be afraid to admit a mistake in this complicated world. This has been a problem with many past presidents. Please have the courage to face up to failed policies, remedy them, and move on.

FISHER STEVENS made his motion picture debut at the age of sixteen in the horror film *The Burning.* But it was *The Flamingo Kid* in 1984 that established Stevens as a serious young actor. Since then, Stevens has starred in such films as *Reversal of Fortune, Short Circuit, Hackers, Only You, Undisputed,* and many others. On the production front, Stevens cofounded the New York–based theater company Naked Angels, which is still going strong after fifteen years. He is also a founding partner of GreeneStreet Films, a New York–based independent film and television production company.

THE CREATIVE COALITION ARCHIVES

Stephen
Collins

Mr. President, I'm no rocket scientist, but I've brought one with me to share my five minutes: John Hagelin, a Harvard-trained quantum physicist who ran for president twice on the Natural Law ticket, understands the science behind some phenomenal research demonstrating that large groups of TM meditators actually have a literal, demonstrable peace-creating effect on the environment. Hagelin can explain this stuff in idiot-proof ways. I'm one of those idiots, and I don't want to cast aspersions on you, but let's just say that Hagelin could explain it to a ten-year-old. You want to fight terrorism? Listen to this.

Some fifty studies that have passed strict peer reviews have shown that we could literally eliminate terrorism, not with armies, but through the energy we generate from our brains during group meditation. You're probably thinking I'm insane and that this is *way* too good to be true, but that's the way Marconi sounded when he first tried to convince the scientific world that sound waves could travel through the air invisibly into his gadget called a radio. My fantasy is that you'll consider creating a cabinet post for Professor Hagelin.

The results produced by temporary groups of meditators lasting weeks or months showed sharp, almost immediate reductions in war deaths averaging better than 70 percent. Most of these studies have been scrutinized by independent scholars, then accepted for publication in academic journals like *The Journal of Conflict Resolution,* published by Yale University.

During days of high attendance by a group of meditators in Jerusalem, war deaths in neighboring Lebanon decreased by 76 percent. During seven different peace-creating assemblies—in a two-year study of the nearly continuous fighting in Lebanon during the 1980s—war deaths decreased by 71 percent. Some of these assemblies were large (seven to eight thousand meditators) and as far away as Fairfield, Iowa—indicating that the peace-creating effect can be felt worldwide.

After reading this research, I wanted to be a foot soldier for peace and took part in two assemblies in Iowa in the early and mid eighties. During the three largest peace-creating assemblies ever held in the West, statistics provided by the Rand Corporation showed a 72 percent reduction in worldwide terrorism. I like thinking I might have been a drop in that bucket.

During the one large peace-creating assembly (eight

thousand meditators) that continued for several years (1988–1990), major conflicts in the world came to an end—including the Soviet invasion of Afghanistan, a seven-year war between Iran and Iraq that had killed millions, and, completely unexpectedly, the Soviet-American Cold War that had threatened us all with nuclear annihilation for forty years.

Independent scholars have been impressed that the findings have often been repeated, are based on available public data, and show an amazing correlation between large groups of meditators and reduced social violence. The possibility of other explanations is mathematically so low as to be insignificant. It sounds woo-woo, but to quote the song: "They all laughed at Christopher Columbus when he said the world was round. . . . "

STEPHEN COLLINS, in a thirty-year career in film, theater, and television, has been featured in plays, miniseries, and movies, including *All the President's Men, Jumpin' Jack Flash,* and *The First Wives Club.* Since 1996, he has starred in the WB series *7th Heaven.* Collins is a founding member of The Creative Coalition and serves on its advisory board.

Richard
Belzer

COURTESY OF NBC UNIVERSAL

Mr. President: I know you are inundated with a lot of requests, but I'd like you to listen to the following quote and consider the information I am about to give you:

> We seek a free flow of information. . . . We are not afraid to entrust the American people with unpleasant facts, foreign ideas, alien philosophies, and competitive values. For a nation that is afraid to let its people judge the truth and falsehood in an open market is a nation that is afraid of its people.
>
> —JOHN F. KENNEDY

Carl Bernstein, the journalist who uncovered the illegal break-in at the Watergate apartments, reported in a famous *Rolling Stone* article in October 1977 that more than four hundred American print and television journalists had secretly acted as operatives or agents for the CIA. Furthermore, to the shock of people at both ends of the political spectrum—those who view with scorn or look with hope to a " liberal media"—Bernstein pointed the finger specifically at the *New York Times,* labeling the paper one of the CIA's most reliable mouthpieces. Two months later, the *Times* leaped to its own defense. Sort of. A *Times* investigation amended Bernstein's count, saying that in actuality there were "more than 800 news and public information organizations and individuals" allied with the CIA. Consequently, they were responsible for only a small percentage of CIA-sponsored news.

Whew! What a relief! Here I was thinking that the *New York Times,* one of the most trusted sources of information in the world, had gotten on its knees for the CIA. But in actuality, the entire information machine—from the most respected figureheads to the lowliest reporters in Bumfuck, Nowhere—are feeding the feds their notes, making connections for the CIA, sharing their sources, and who-knows-what-else. It's like finding out that your wife has been sleeping with your best friend. Then having her tell you, "Hey—don't sweat it. I've also been sleeping with your best friend's father, your best friend's mechanic, your best friend's proctologist, and your best friend's dog. Your best friend doesn't mean a thing to me."

Mr. President, taking all that into consideration, please let me and the American people know where we can learn the truth and whom we can trust. With all due respect, I expect an answer on my desk in the morning.

Thanking you in advance, from a curious and loving Jew.

RICHARD BELZER, author, actor, and executive producer, currently stars as Detective John Munch in NBC's *Law and Order: Special Victims Unit.* He has worked in everything from off-Broadway to morning radio to feature films. He was the executive producer of *Bitter Jester,* a behind-the-scenes look at the life of a stand-up comic, and is the author of the book *UFOs, JFK, and Elvis: Conspiracies You Don't Have to Be Crazy to Believe.* Belzer serves on The Creative Coalition's board of directors.

David Henry Hwang

CRAIG SCHWARTZ

Mr. President, I would like to talk to you about the unfortunate demise of a once-promising movement: multiculturalism. In the 1990s, multiculturalism became a target of derision in certain circles. Right-wing commentators cagily exploited the term *political correctness* to demonize a movement that sought to empower various groups whose viewpoints and experiences had previously been ignored or patronized. Multiculturalism's primary thrust was to shatter the notion of a single immutable reality: people perceive the world differently from the standpoint of their different cultures and communities. As multiculturalism evolved from the ethnic power and feminist movements of the 1960s and 1970s, however, its proponents sometimes fell prey to excesses of rhetoric and practice. By the turn of the millennium, even an early advocate such as myself had started to perceive the movement as worn-out, its precepts dated.

Multiculturalism, though historically necessary, had perhaps outlived its usefulness. All this changed for me on September 11, 2001.

As our nation struggled to respond to a newly effective terrorist movement, multiculturalism took on renewed relevance. In the twenty-first century, its tenets could serve not only to advance the rights of minorities and women domestically, but also as a lens through which to evaluate our national defense strategies. The men who drove the planes into the Twin Towers were neither greedy nor insane; they did so because their cultural vantage point caused them to see an entirely different world than the one most of us see. They were fundamentalists—"uniculturalists" who believed that their vision of reality constituted an absolute truth, and that those who disagreed were less than human.

It is a terrible mistake to fight fundamentalism with fundamentalism, because this leaves no middle ground where competing realities can struggle for tolerance. In order to stop terrorists, we must first appreciate, if not their actions, at least the cultures and experiences that breed them. Only then can we devise strategies that effectively counter the more violent manifestations of their realities. Multiculturalism is profoundly antifundamentalist; it rejects the notion of a single absolute truth that all humans should hold. This recognition is the first step to understanding our enemies.

The United States lost the war in Vietnam largely because it was unable or unwilling to understand that the Vietcong saw themselves as nationalists first, Communists second. Similarly, the current administration has utterly failed to apply the lessons of multiculturalism to its war on terrorism. Instead, it places faith in its own fundamentalisms, which have paved a road to disaster. Only those unable to see past their own cultural biases could have imagined that Iraqis would welcome American occupiers as liberators. Only a uniculturalist administration would have arrogantly dismissed the world community's well-founded objections. Only leaders truly insensitive to cultural differences would think to stop an Arab named bin Laden by attacking another named Hussein.

I am asking for an American president who will fight terrorism vigilantly, which means fighting it wisely. In order to reach those who hate us, we must first understand the realities of their cultures. Multiculturalism can serve as a valuable tool for national security in our current brave new world.

DAVID HENRY HWANG's plays include *M. Butterfly, Golden Child, The Dance and the Railroad,* and *FOB.* He also coauthored, with Elton John and Tim Rice, the international hit musical *Aida.*

Christie
Hefner

Mr. President: Please allow me to begin with a quote: "Congress shall make no law respecting an establishment of religion, or prohibiting the free exercise thereof; or abridging the freedom of speech, or of the press; or the right of the people peaceably to assemble, and to petition the Government for a redress of grievances." The origins of this statement can be traced to a bill introduced by Thomas Jefferson. With some changes proposed by James Madison, it became law in 1786. That's such a long time ago, Mr. President, that you would think this very first amendment to our Constitution would no longer be in peril, or even a matter of debate. But in the wake of the terrorist attacks in this country, it is again coming under pressure. I ask, Mr. President, that you always bear in mind that the war we are waging is a war of ideas as much as a war of weapons. And that the free expression of ideas, including the right to dissent, is the hallmark of an open, democratic society. Moreover, for our citizens and the citizens of other countries to have confidence in our actions and our motives, we need to do all we can to make our government transparent and open. Let's open government to both the letter and the spirit of our First Amendment such that all voices are heard, grievances addressed, and ideas explored. Our best exports are democracy, freedom, and pluralism. You are in the most powerful position to further those values through your use of the bully pulpit, executive orders, legislative direction, and judicial nominees.

CHRISTIE HEFNER is chairman and chief executive officer of Playboy Enterprises. She is also active in a number of organizations, and has received many awards, including the 1990 Eleanor Roosevelt Award for her commitment to human rights and civil liberties. Hefner serves on the advisory boards of The Creative Coalition and the American Civil Liberties Union.

Frances
Fisher

ALLISON CANE

Hello, Mr. President . . . Let's talk about women's rights. Some people seem to think it has nothing to do with them. "It's a female thing," I have heard. Or, "What does that have to do with me?"

We all have mothers. We all came from women. Whether they abandoned us, or were terrible, or were deeply caring and loving, I believe a mother, more often than not, is the most influential force in a person's life. And to me, that is why women's rights are important to each and every human being on this planet.

I never learned about competition until I started playing sports in junior high, and I learned that there was a "winning" team and a "losing" team. Competition was something I felt was manufactured. And when I grew into my teen years, I saw how society and the media influenced people to compete with one another, personally and professionally; the playing field opened up into a way of life, but I never bought into it.

Then, when I had my child, I sat in a circle with other mothers and their babies, and do you know what we did? We taught our children how to cooperate with one another. We taught our children how to share. We taught our children how to communicate.

That is what mothers do. That is what women instinctively know is right.

So, Mr. President, what does this have to do with women's rights?

You know the quote "The hand that rocks the cradle rules the world." A mother who has a child whom she wants will do everything she can to nurture, educate, and send into the world the best example of her mothering possible. A mother who has a child whom she doesn't want, for whatever reason, will unconsciously create havoc in that child's life. Yes, she can love that child, but there are psychological threads that weave a web so insidious that, well, it's the therapist's task to untangle, now isn't it?

The only reason for a woman to bring a child into the world is that she wants that child. To force a woman to carry a child against her will is, first of all, nobody's right, and second, and in my opinion, it is a moral crime, because that unwanted child will grow up most likely to play out his twisted perception of life, influenced by a mother who had no desire for him in the first place.

Perhaps you think I am too radical, but I believe that

most of the problems in the world have been caused by people who never learned (from their mothers) how to cooperate.

I am asking that you do everything in your power to provide education about reproduction to every human being in our country, and on this planet. I am asking you to make sure that the laws of the United States allow a woman to make her own decision whether she wants to have a child or not, and that nobody and no laws come between any woman and her American right to "life, liberty, and the pursuit of happiness."

FRANCES FISHER's Hollywood career has spanned more than two decades and includes over a hundred credits. Among her television and film credits are *Lucy and Desi: Before the Laughter, Law & Order, Laws of Attraction,* and *Titanic.*

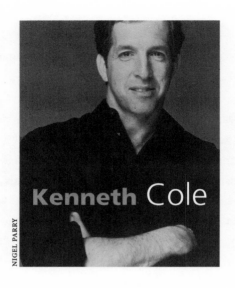

Kenneth Cole

NIGEL PARRY

Mr. President: I was once taught that a principal role of government was to serve those among us least able to serve themselves—the proverbial safety net. Somehow, about twenty years ago, at the time of the first Reagan administration, something seems to have changed, and has continued to do so since. The safety net continues to develop more and more holes. Today, as a matter of policy and philosophy, the idea is promoted that government functions best when it is small and minimally involved in the lives of people. We are also no longer supposed to look to government to help correct injustices or inefficiencies in American business, education, and society, but rather to look to the private sector and the free markets. Don't put your faith in government, we are told, but in the notion that good will trickle down to solve what is not good. Why do we think this should work? Has it ever worked before? Why shouldn't all of the haves, who are seeking to have more, be further enabled, even if it is at the expense of the have-nots? It seems we want all the government we need but no more than the government we need—the catchphrase of the day. And it is clearly working well. Unless, of course, you have needs. Or in other words, the system is working well for those who don't need the system.

Consider that 3.5 million Americans—almost 40 percent of them children—experience homelessness every year. This in a country that has as much abundance as any other, and more than it has ever had. We are a trillion dollars weaker than we were four years ago, because of questionable appropriated tax cuts and hundreds of billions of dollars spent on a questionably appropriate war in Iraq. A fraction of that could solve much of this and many other domestic problems. How do we spend so extravagantly chasing a mirage so far away when the evidence of mass homelessness is in front of our eyes every day? With all due respect, Mr. President, why am I getting a $600 check in the mail when so many others beg for quarters? Is it for me to trickle it down to them? Is that the most effective way to help those with less? Do you know that rescinding your tax cut for just the richest 1 percent of Americans would raise $87 billion?

Those sleeping on the streets and in public parks are not the end of America's dispossessed. Forty-one thousand Americans died of AIDS last year, and 42 million people around the world are living with it. By the year

2010 there could be as many as 100 million people world-wide infected with HIV/AIDS. If there is truly a global economy, then there is most certainly a global community. How do we put our heads on our pillows at night knowing that we are not doing all that we can?

When three thousand people died in the terrible events of 9/11, every bit of this country's resources was mobilized overnight to fight an enemy who is nearly invisible and, I might add, still at large. We leveraged our international credibility in an effort to make what we felt was a commensurate response. That very day, Mr. President, a very visible enemy struck an estimated fourteen thousand citizens of the world. And that amount of people contract HIV every day. And they will all die of AIDS, unless, of course, there is a cure. We know this enemy, we know where it lives, and we know where to find it. We have to mobilize and invest in a vaccine to prevent HIV and another to cure AIDS. We have to do whatever it takes at any cost, just as we have done to fight global terrorism. But this terrorism, sir, admits of no diplomacy. It takes merely courage, commitment, and money, which we seem to find when only certain of us are perceived to be at risk.

America has made a measured commitment to fighting HIV/AIDS, which is fine if we had the time for such calculated and measured steps. But we don't have time to take measured steps. We must act, now, for both the people in our streets and those suffering from the scourge of possibly the greatest plague of all time.

So, Mr. President, I urge you to enable this government to truly be one: of the people and for *all* the people, and I thank you for your time.

KENNETH COLE is the founder, chairman, CEO, and chief creative director of Kenneth Cole Productions, Inc., a public company with a social conscience that manufactures and distributes footwear, clothing, fragrance, and accessories for women, men, and children, with retail stores in seventeen countries. He is a member of The Creative Coalition's advisory board.

Chris Cooper

If I had five minutes to spend with the president, I would ask him why the current administration is dismantling the Individuals with Disabilities Education Act (IDEA), when even with this act fully in place we had to hire a lawyer to get our severely disabled son a "free and appropriate public school education." The administration has pushed for more "accountability" while taking federal pressure off of states for compliance. The bill to "reform" the original IDEA received more dissenting votes in the House of Representatives than any special-education bill in history and was vehemently opposed by almost every disability organization. However, the bill passed. Now the Senate has approved its own version. I would hope the Senate is listening to those who advocate for children and adults with special needs, but their version puts an undue burden on parents to understand and report their child's disability very early lest they not qualify. I appeal to the president, who must sign whatever legislation may emerge, to listen to the advocates for the disabled, who have only the children's interest at heart. I ask you further why is it that we now have a system in which my sixteen-year-old son, a straight-A student, will not receive a diploma. The federal and state mandates for testing to be the sole arbiter of requirement for a diploma LEAVES OUR SON BEHIND. This is grossly unfair. I would also want to know why, after the great fanfare of announcing "No Child Left Behind," this mandate remains unfunded.

CHRIS COOPER was recognized in 2003 with an Academy Award and a Golden Globe Award for best supporting actor for his portrayal of John Laroche in *Adaptation*, written by Charlie Kaufman and directed by Spike Jonze. He will next be seen in *Silver City*, directed by John Sayles. Cooper will shortly begin filming *Conquistadora*, written by Marianne Leone (his wife) and starring Patricia Clarkson. Other film credits include *Lone Star*, *Seabiscuit*, *The Bourne Identity*, and *Matewan*.

Tom
Arnold

Dear Mr. President: Please don't lie to me, and if you cannot tell me the truth, say so. If it's about the oil, say it's about the oil. Please make brave decisions, not based on polls; after all, I count on you to be smarter than me. Global warming and mercury in our fish are real and you know it. Know that it's better to be respected than feared. Realize that our form of democracy is not for everyone. Do things to give hope to children, not just in America but in Palestine, Iraq, everywhere when possible. When you screw up, apologize—I will probably forgive you and will definitely respect you more. Please consider the other side and try to understand why they feel the way they do. Don't do anything to take freedoms away from anyone. Before sending anyone to war, ask yourself, "Would I go? Would I send my parents? My children?" Be noble and fearless, never a hypocrite, and never, never, never lose your sense of humor. Like a good father, let me know that everything is going to be okay so I can sleep at night. Protect our freedom of speech, and since there is no better word to describe bullshit than bullshit, please take that off the official forbidden-words list.

TOM ARNOLD, one of the hosts of Fox SportsNet's *The Best Damn Sports Show Period,* has starred in numerous feature films and television shows. His movie credits include *Nine Months, True Lies,* and *Soul Plane.* Arnold has also produced and written for television.

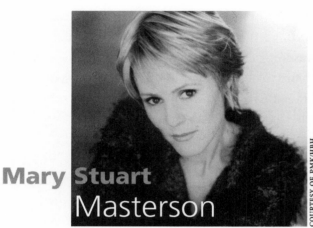

Mary Stuart
Masterson

COURTESY OF PMK/HBH

If I had five minutes with the next president of the United States, I would suggest that all meetings with international leaders be conducted after they had given massages to one another. The actual meetings would be carried out in the nude. Marijuana should be legalized and taxed. All taxes collected from weed should be used to treat victims of abuse, which are usually related to alcohol. All Americans should be paid a living wage and have no less than two months off per year. Reality shows should be banned from television in favor of people actually living their own reality. Citizens' votes should be counted—even those of black citizens in Florida. Politics should stop being so political. We don't have much time to save our country from absolute ruin. We have to get together on some big stuff.

So, Madame President, what do you plan to do to save

our reputation? At this moment, we are considered arrogant opportunists across much of the globe. We are the necessary evil to our trading partners and the infidel to our enemies. Our shell game of proxy wars is no different from that played by imperialist nations before us. But we do have a different agenda, at least in part. And that is what I want you, as my president, to get right before we lose our great country. We really do have a set of ideals worth sharing. That doesn't mean we can bully our way across the globe committing a version of corporate rape on vulnerable nations who have something we want, and do it in the name of our moral imperative. I know we really do mean to bring democracy to the people of Iraq, and they seem to need it. I know we had to stop the genocide in Kosovo. But it happened in Rwanda and we did nothing. It happened in the Congo and we did nothing. So, what are the real criteria for our participation in these wars? Let's be honest about it. It's corporate hegemony, baby.

The fact that we are more interested in extreme makeovers and the last episode of *Friends* (of which I am a fan, by the way) than hearing what our armed forces did to prisoners of war in an Iraqi prison tells me we've checked out. Americans need to be engaged in the process of their own citizenry. After the last election, I can see why people no longer think their voices are being heard. Their votes aren't even being counted.

Let's deal with the war on terror by getting at the root cause. They don't like us because we're fat, happy, entitled, and take whatever we want from whomever we want because we can. It won't last forever. We are living in a time when our global interdependence makes us more vulnerable than ever before. Our dependence on foreign oil and our unwillingness to change it is the most obvious of our vulnerabilities. But what about our total dependence on China and Indonesia? We need China as much, if not more, than they need us, and they are getting their economic ducks in a row. We need India to process our taxes and our most sensitive intelligence data. None of the above countries has a huge middle class like we do. But what happens when they do? If the average Chinese or Indian person demands the kind of middle-class lifestyle we've come to feel entitled to enjoy, we will start to regret the fact that we have allowed our farmland to be lost to preventable soil erosion. We will regret that we allowed the entire southwestern United States to build condos in deserts in the erroneous belief that there was an unlimited supply of water from the dammed Colorado River to keep their lawns watered and their swimming pools filled. We will wish we had demanded that a certain amount of new homes use alternative sources of energy and be built to high efficiency code. In short, we will be out of luck because we will have used up all our stuff. If we had been paying attention before we killed off most of the Native Americans, we would have learned a valuable lesson about land use versus the delusional concept of "ownership." The tribal elders sure would have had a laugh to hear that advertisers were trying to get the "rights" to beam laser advertisements on the moon for Earth's global consumption.

Madame President, will you help restore us to sanity? We have become so arrogant in our dealings with the world that we allow ourselves to set the worst kind of example for democracy. By some estimates, we use 25 percent of the world's natural resources although we have only 4 percent of the world's population. That may work for a little while longer, but it can't continue forever. We must set an example by participating in future environmental summits like the one in Johannesburg we barely attended last year.

We have created our enemies over and over again only to find ourselves under their attack. We are hypocrites in the eyes of many nations around the world because we have repeatedly abandoned the welfare of our own country in favor of fighting proxy wars wherever our imperialist economic interests are imperiled. For the first time in my life, I genuinely feel my country is in grave danger. Not only because of the real threats we face from terrorists, but because our education, health care, and environmental ethics have been left to decay as we spend more and more money on shell games like the war in Iraq. Our country is founded on the greatest principles imaginable and it works really well. I am proud to be an American. I am grateful for the sacrifices the armed forces have undergone to protect my freedom. I feel lucky to have been born in a country where freedoms are protected by law and diversity is celebrated. Still, I wish the rest of the world knew that we're really pretty cool and we want to get along.

Madame President, would you please add some compassionate liberalism to the White House and run this nation more like a family and less like a corporation whose only concern is for the bottom line? I really want to be able to travel to Europe this summer and I am too embarrassed to go to France. Thank you for your time.

> *I should like to be able to love my country and still love justice.*
>
> —ALBERT CAMUS

MARY STUART MASTERSON's off-Broadway credits include Horton Foote's *Lily Dale* and Beth Henley's *The Lucky Spot*. Her more than twenty-five films include *Fried Green Tomatoes, Benny and Joon,* and *Some Kind of Wonderful.* She is a board member of Rainforest Alliance and the Actors Studio.

Tim
Matheson

Mr. President: In my view, the definition of a leader is one who is proactive and out in front on an issue, who leads by strength of inquiry, analysis, and reflection, and who has the courage to make decisions while fully understanding the importance of consensus. Right now, we are being reactive in the world. Our character and our response to 9/11 has become distinctly un-American in tone. Traditionally, America has been the leader in being stalwart and true to its principles, especially in terms of international cooperation, but now it seems we have fallen prey to revenge and vindictiveness, which has lately escalated into the abuse of people in our custody. I would encourage you, our president, to return to the principles this country was founded on.

We must return to diplomacy as a means to enact change in the world. We must use our power and influence in a manner that is not inflammatory and divisive, but wise and unifying. We must seek to play a leading and helpful role in brokering peace. Our self-interests should everywhere be on the side of peace, whether in the Middle East, the Koreas, or with respect to India and Pakistan. We are often pilloried for pursuing our self-interests abroad; if we understood that prosperity cannot be had without peace, we could plead guilty to having our own agenda, and rightfully so. As long as peace is the first order of the day, we are on the right side of things.

Mr. President, whatever our actions abroad, they must not be unilateral. We have paid an enormous price—morally, diplomatically, and economically—for being willing to go it alone with our patchwork "coalition."

Ultimately, in seeking vengeance for the terrible things that happened on our soil in 2001, we have lost sight of some of the tenets upon which international relations are based. Rights have been abridged at home, but we, understandably, are under our highest security alert. Although we must be vigilant about excesses, we should be most concerned about overreacting in countries not our own. We may have gone too far already in our reactions. It is time for proactivity, confronting the changing reality as it has been revealed to us, not going it alone, but with a wide international consensus. Much of the world is interested in peace. Peace is a good business to be in.

TIM MATHESON, actor, director, and producer, has come a long way since his breakout role in the comedy classic *Animal House.* Through a succession of film and television acting roles, as well as numerous directing and producing projects, Matheson has embraced his craft from both sides of the camera.

Kathy
Najimy

MICHAEL LAMONT

Well, depending on who the president is, I would either slap him or French-kiss him. Then I would usher him into a helicopter standing conveniently by. I would pull my hair back in a clip so it wouldn't get all mussed, like Sandra Bullock in *Speed*.

First, we would fly over something impressive like the Grand Canyon just so he thinks we're on a joyride, and right when he's thinking, "Oh great . . . a sky tour . . . how fun!" I would take him over a small home in, oh, let's say . . . Alabama. And we would look down on a fifteen-year-old girl about to die from an illegal abortion. . . .

Then maybe we'd fly right over a health clinic to see someone from the ridiculous right shoot a health-care provider on her way in to work. Again, I would then apologize for getting so intense before lunch and maybe I would offer him a sandwich or some of my mom's tabouleh before we flew on.

I would then take him over the house of a family who has lost a son or a daughter in the war in Iraq. Maybe we'd watch several families gather and mourn the loss of their brother or sister or husband or wife or mother or father who flew over to some country that we were not invited into . . . a soldier who had either been forced to go or convinced it was the right thing to do. I would turn on Fox News (on my wrist TV) and then we . . . well, I would talk about how not receiving the whole truth, but rather censored, faux-patriotic bits of the real global news encourages the rampant racism/ignorance in this country, how it fuels the rage of war and justifies needless deaths.

Maybe then it would be time for us to announce the weather and traffic on some AM radio station. We would call ourselves "Jamie and Bean." Then we would fly over the sea and I would ask him to count with me how many oily dead birds were washed ashore. We would marvel at the trash. At this point I would politely apologize for the bummer trip and offer him a Diet Coke. Then we would fly over the downtown area of, well, almost any city in America, and watch the homeless and hungry walking the streets. We would watch the children the longest. And we would try not to look away. For our last final minutes I would like to do two things. . . . Land in the parking lot of an AIDS hospice and go in just for a minute to sing Lainie Kazan songs to the men and women lying in there. Have him sign a few autographs . . . I mean he *is* the president, right? Finally, I would hover over Central Park in Manhattan and find a couple . . . a same-sex couple. One that has been together for, oh, maybe twenty years . . . and simply look at them holding hands. Hands with no rings. Then it would be time for a final snack, a thank-you, maybe a hug (again, depending upon who it is), and then one of those exciting drop-offs out of the chopper down a rope to his pad. I would wave to him out the window of the helicopter and yell, "Please don't forget the talk we had about Oprah and Hillary!!!!!" . . . and taking my last gulp of Diet Coke . . . I would fly away.

KATHY NAJIMY has appeared in more than twenty films, and is best known for her work in *Sister Act* and *Hocus Pocus.* Her TV work includes three seasons on *Veronica's Closet;* her stage work includes a Broadway run in *Dirty Blonde.* As a star of her original feminist play *The Kathy and Mo Show,* she appeared for several years onstage and in two HBO specials.

Eric
McCormack

NBC (CHRIS HASTON)

Mr. President: I know He's a friend of yours, but God has got to go. Not completely gone, you understand. He's still the boss in churches and synagogues and mosques, still a welcome guest at dinner tables and weddings, but He's got to get the hell out of the White House. If there ever was a separation of church and state, it is now a separation of inches, a thin veil. God didn't run for office, but more and more He seems to be making the decisions we've left in the hands of our elected officials.

This might be acceptable if we all agreed on and believed in the same God. But in a country where Jew disagrees with Jew, Muslim with Muslim, and there are seemingly thirty-one flavors of Christian, how can the Lord ever be used as a political divining rod? Hell, the heartland is made up of dozens of small towns where white Christians still segregate themselves from black

Christians. This may be one nation but it isn't under one God. And for a lot of voters, it isn't under any god.

Our political decisions have to be made with a sober, secular eye, influenced only by human empathy, not by ancient prejudice and debatable scripture. I mean, how are *we* different from *them?* We think it's crazy when a suicide bomber blows himself up for Allah, yet hardly blink when our elected leader announces we are fighting a "crusade." We are all appalled at the age-old treatment of women in much of the Third World, but deny an American woman's right to choose by quoting the Bible. We pride ourselves on equal rights and justice for all, yet denounce gay marriage because, let's face it, most of the right wing thinks the gays are going to burn in hell.

This is no way to run a railroad, theirs or ours. Government, like the law, must operate on hearts and minds and leave the soul at home. It's in your best interests, after all . . . I mean, God wouldn't want anyone to own guns, right? At least mine wouldn't.

ERIC McCORMACK was born in Toronto in 1963 and became an American citizen in 1999. In 2001, he won an Emmy for his portrayal of Will Truman on NBC's *Will and Grace.*

Lauren Holly

Here are the questions I would ask the president, given the chance.

Mr. President, would you please allow the administering of truth serum before we begin?

Thank you.

[A little small talk here to let the serum take effect . . .]

Mr. President, why do you want to be president?

Who convinced you that you could or should be president?

Why do you think you are qualified to be president?

Let's talk about gasoline. Can you explain why the price of gas seems to go up just before an election? Am I wrong?

Is the presidency really a solo office or is it ruled by committee?

Who's on the committee?

Do you go to bed every night feeling fulfilled, or is it just a day of concessions for you?

Let's talk about terrorism. *[This is where I really hope the serum is kicking in. . . .]* What is the real threat of terrorism?

Is there stuff that we don't know about?

Is there stuff that *I* don't know about?

Are you afraid?

[We drink water.]

Who is more organized, the Republicans or the Democrats?

Why don't I know who the real John Kerry is?

Why do I feel like I know George Bush?

Is that a good thing?

Mr. President, my whole theory is that our social skills and philosophy of life are developed in kindergarten, where there are people we like and people we don't like, and it's all clear and everyone is in the same class. Then we forget all that and make things complicated and our skills fail us and we don't know whom we like and whom we don't like and people get into warring groups.

Do you think that?

Do you like what we have?

You can talk now.

LAUREN HOLLY, accomplished film and television actress, can also list the credits of writer and producer on her diverse résumé. Holly has worked nonstop since her breakthrough performance in the box-office smash *Dumb and Dumber.* Her other credits include *Spirited Away, Any Given Sunday, Sabrina, Turbulence, Beautiful Girls, Dragon: The Bruce Lee Story, A Smile Like Yours, Down Periscope, Entropy, The Last Producer, What Women Want,* and the Emmy Award–winning series *Picket Fences* and *Chicago Hope.*

Alan
Cumming

Mr. President: You must forgive me for my audacity in writing this. I am not one of your citizens, although I do reside in your country. But worry not. I am not one of those illegal immigrants who are so vilified at election times in your border states to scare the electorate into voting against any wishy-washy liberals who might actually allow these people in and give them rights or benefits, instead of the much more sensible alternative of letting them work illegally at raising the children and keeping the homes of America, or any of the other low-paid jobs that no sensible American would want to do.

No, be not alarmed. I am a legal resident. I am just an alien. And not one of the new breed of aliens we have all sadly had to become more wary of since the horrible events of 2001. Relax, I am not dark-skinned, though I am European. And I only wear a towel in public at the gym, and if I did have a God (I don't mean to alarm you, but I don't think She exists) it wouldn't be a nasty, war-mongering one like Allah or one of those other ones that demand constant kneeling and regular slashing of oneself with chains and the like.

No, no, no. I am an alien of extraordinary ability, which in spite of its rather ominous overtones of espionage and such like, really means that I am an actor who was asked to work in your country and liked it and stayed.

Since I have lived here, there have been two presidents, and so my understanding of your job, be it naive and simplistic, is entirely gleaned from their examples.

So here, Mr. President, are a few tips: You may have had, no doubt, a family member remove thousands of people from the electoral register to enable your ascension to power, but please don't forget to be publicly outraged when other countries do exactly the same thing. And oh yes, don't ever comment on the matter even when your own people admit that the margin of error involved in this "cleansing" translates into many thousands more votes than your opponent lost by.

Forgive me if I am preaching to the choir here, but remember to start a war without sufficient evidence of any just cause to do so, apart from the fact that you just don't seem to like dark-skinned people (call them "evil folks" when you don't want to get bogged down with specifics, by the way), and tell your public that you have top-secret evidence that certain countries with really large fuel supplies are about to launch nuclear bombs, but be careful to turn a blind eye to countries like India and Pakistan when they threaten to do so because of course they don't have much fuel to take. Actually, come to think of it, don't mention nuclear bombs; they're too hard to pronounce. You don't want to look stupid.

What else? Oh yes, make inappropriate jokes whenever you can; encourage your countrymen to believe certain evil folks are in utter cahoots when in fact they don't like one another at all; claim any minor and normal upward fluctuation in the world's economy as proof that all your policies, not just the economic ones, are working great.

I think you'll find it's best to have had a drug problem of some kind in the past, or at least to admit to having had drugs but not having consumed them in the way of most mortal men. Have offspring who are either so ridiculously successful that they can inspire jealous rage, or else drunk yahoos who give stupid Americans a bad name.

If you aren't really charismatic and sexy, with a series of messy public extramarital affairs behind you, including lying under oath that a love affair with a young, impressionable woman never happened, then go the other way altogether and cultivate a look that is more prairie dog than horn dog, talk a lot about Texas, and if possible— but this might be milking the jock sympathy vote a little too far—try asphyxiating on a bar snack whilst watching sports alone.

Make sure you either court the gay vote by allying

yourself with lots of queer causes and maybe even putting out a rumor that your wife is a lipstick lesbian OR completely alienate them and hopefully ensnare another group of minority voters (they being fascists) by denying gays the same basic rights and benefits as all your other citizens.

Finally, Mr. President—and by the way, thank you; I know you don't have to listen to anyone, least of all someone like me, for this length of time—never, ever admit you are wrong.

It's always *their* fault.

Don't ask why, ask how.

Oh, and have the same name as a previous president—even if it's your dad.

ALAN CUMMING was trained at the Royal Scottish Academy of Music and Drama. On the New York stage he has appeared in *Elle* (which he also adapted), *Design for Living,* and *Cabaret.* Recent films include *Eyes Wide Shut, Emma, Circle of Friends,* and *Goldeneye.* He is currently filming Showtime's *Reefer Madness.*

CHARLES D. ROBISON

Peter Yarrow

First, congratulations! You could rescue our country, but it will not be an easy job, no matter how gifted and passionate, fair-handed, and distinguished a leader you are.

Know that your countrymen and countrywomen are wounded and filled with mistrust. They have, in large part, become cynical about the motivations of others, and many will be cynical about what they perceive you, and your objectives, to be. So listen to them, but know that you are frequently listening to the voices of people who are yearning to trust, but are afraid to do so lest they be lied to and betrayed once again. Give them your heart and they will begin to believe in you and themselves once again. Together, you can restore the heart of America and make it strong once again.

Make sure you examine and understand the issues in depth. Also, you must share your reasons for making such decisions, in depth, so that Americans will be reengaged in the essential dialogue of democracy and honor it with their thoughtful, constructive debate.

Promise only what you can reasonably expect to accomplish, and then deliver it, if at all possible, both in substance and in degree.

Never use the tragedies of our nation to frighten America for your political gain. Never politicize your nation's pain to create "blank-check" authority for yourself and your administration. Never stifle the dialogue that is the lifeblood of democracy by accusing those who disagree with your politics of being unpatriotic or disloyal.

By example and through your leadership, teach tolerance, acceptance, and respect. Refrain from sarcasm and ridicule. Be a conciliator and a healer. Never try to bully other nations. If you do, more and more, America will be hated and feared.

Stay the course of your mission, but be flexible enough to change tactics and strategies when the facts, or conditions, change.

Do not let the media govern your responses or policies. Listen, but stay independent in your judgment. Always be open, but stay clear of voices from your God, or any other person's God, in your political decision-making process. America is not a theocracy.

Tell the American people that the buck stops with you and take responsibility for those whom you have chosen to serve with you. Be strong enough and humble enough to admit when you or your advisers have made a mistake.

Redress the economic unfairness that has plagued the soul of this nation. Tax those who have more, and give back to those who deserve the support of a fair and compassionate government, a government that truly represents the American dream of fairness and equal opportunity.

Appoint fair-minded jurists to the Supreme Court so as to prevent the erosion of our constitutional rights.

Restore hard-won environmental projects and initiatives. Make sure America signs the Global Warming Treaty, leads other nations in its observance, and signs other such international treaties.

Move America toward being a land of equal opportunity, by making sure that all children receive an equal amount of funding and resources for their education.

Change the nation's educational paradigm so that the development of children's character is treated with the same seriousness as the development of their academic and intellectual capacities. Make sure educators know that their charge is to teach the whole child; both sides of the report card. Let children be taught to respect themselves, and one another, for their inherent worth, rather than for the empty priorities of fame, money, and power. This is the sure, and only, way to build peace in the world.

Honor our teachers, who, aside from America's parents, are the most important determinants of our future. If teachers are properly honored and respected, then the next generation of Americans will be more generous, more sincere, more involved, more caring, and more respectful than we are.

Focus the justice system on prisoner reform, crime prevention, and building community, as opposed to punishment and retribution. Reassess our sentencing laws, and see what can be done to properly and safely grant probation to those who were incarcerated under draconian laws from a previous time. Use your powers of presidential pardon, if necessary in new ways, to effect this change. Stop the building of new jails and start building new schools.

End the savage treatment of those put in detention or jail without due process, especially those who are foreign born, and recognize that America must stand for, and practice, the observance of freedom, in war and in peace. Scrupulously observe the conventions of Geneva and other international agreements governing prisoners of war, and never flout the rule or spirit of the law.

Never go to war without declaring war and making sure that America wages war only as a last and most regrettable resort—after all diplomatic and peaceful means of resolution are completely and utterly exhausted.

Consider the plight of those who have nothing to live for, or else such people will become easy targets for mass mobilization by terrorists. Then we will have no option but to become a country that is one huge, gated society, one that must protect its citizens by abbreviating or eliminating our rights. Then we will cease to be a democracy. Your leadership can prevent this decline of America into an Orwellian state and/or the triggering of Armageddon.

The time is now, Mr. President. Good luck and God-speed.

PETER YARROW is a performer-activist whose work with Peter, Paul, and Mary has put him on the front lines of the efforts for social justice and human rights for more than four decades. Operation Respect: Don't Laugh at Me, a nonprofit he founded in 1999, is a leader in the movement to establish safe, respectful environments for children in schools and communities.

GLORIA RODRIGUEZ

Garland
Jeffreys

I distrust political parties with all my heart and am sickened by how much money is spent in support of the election of politicians who in the end ignore the real needs of Americans. Elections are an opportunity for the people to vote for true public servants. Yet it seems to me that politicians don't really have much to do with regular people. They appear to be more interested in taking care of their own. The tax cuts that have been instituted, for example, are clearly a benefit to the privileged.

If I were going to sit down with the president, I'd ask him or her to demonstrate that he or she really cares about people in this country as opposed to just paying lip service to the idea of caring. What would really be the evidence? To finally do something about health care. It is just an outrageous thing that in a country of so much wealth there are more than fifty million people without health insurance.

As for world events, the idiocy of this intervention in Iraq has cost us an incredible amount of money and human life on both sides. It is simply insane when you think of all the money that is now unavailable for services that are truly helpful to people in need in America.

We are still separated by race and religion. We have not repaired the past, and we're still divided by prejudice that threatens our future. I want a president who will truly stand, in word and in deed, for the dream of every American: equal rights for one and all.

Real, honest, and forthright action programs for education (ones that are, yes, about money) are in order. We should pay teachers what they are worth. We must make teaching a career that appeals to the talented, committed, and visionary among us who can make such a huge difference in our children's lives. I was once a teacher in elementary school. I could see the roots of dysfunction right there in front of me—kids with bruises, kids with too much on their minds about what was going on at home, kids who were hungry, poorly dressed, coming from chaos.

If we really were in fact paying attention to the people of our country, we would not only not miss those problems, but would be determined to do *all* that we could to eliminate them. And then we might think twice about educating the rest of the world to our way of life. Let's share the wealth of wisdom here at home; let's make life better for all Americans first.

***

GARLAND JEFFREYS's thoughtful, passionate songs mix rock and roll, soul, reggae, garage, doo-wop, and Latin influences to create a deeply personal hybrid that reflects his own multiethnic roots. A New York native and an icon of the music scene for the last thirty-five years, Garland is presently working on several new recordings.

GREG GORMAN

Patricia
Hearst

I would like to propose a constitutional amendment to abolish what Thomas Jefferson once called "the most dangerous blot on our Constitution"—the Electoral College. I think it is the biggest fraud ever perpetrated on the American people. Every four years people go to the polls imagining they are voting for a president. In fact, they are voting for "electors"—citizens who are empowered to cast all their state's votes for the single candidate who receives the most votes.

The president of the United States is the only elected official who is not elected in a direct election, meaning "one man, one vote." Many people don't understand how this happened.

Two centuries ago the Constitutional Convention considered many ways to select the president of the emerging republic, from popular election to assigning the decision to the Congress. The Electoral College was a compromise that reflected a basic mistrust of the electorate—the same mistrust that denied the vote to women, African-Americans, and people who did not own property. The establishment of the Electoral College ensured that should the electorate vote for an "unsuitable" candidate, the electors could legally alter the outcome by electing a "suitable" president.

Today, the number of votes each state has in the Electoral College is the same as the number of representatives it has in Congress. As a result, the states with the greatest population have the most electoral votes, and therefore carry the most weight in the electoral process as it exists. Moreover, it is a winner-take-all system, and the candidate who wins the state, even by a single vote, receives all that state's electoral votes. In theory, since it takes 270 votes out of a total of 538 to secure the presidency, a candidate could triumph by winning a dozen heavily populated states. If you happen to live in a state that votes overwhelmingly for the Republican Party (or vice versa), you may as well not waste your time voting. True, you may be lured to the polls by other important election issues that day, but voting for "president" is a waste of a chad.

This goes triple if you imagine that voting for a third-party candidate is making a political statement. The system is rigged against you. You have no voice. You are completely disenfranchised! The Founding Fathers were extremely biased in favor of a two-party system and everything's working just the way it was intended when it comes to you.

It's time for America to truly become a democracy—the kind we would be proud to export! One man, one vote! Abolish the Electoral College!

PATRICIA HEARST is an actress and author.

Bob
Balaban

LEE SALEM

Dear Next Mr. President: In the eyes of the rest of the world it seems as if so much of our rhetoric is just convenient posturing. I can imagine what an impossible job being president will be, and I certainly don't envy you. But sometimes I think the president forgets that people really pay attention to what he says, and that we can pretty quickly decide whether he is speaking truthfully.

A small example: It is horrendous that Nicholas Berg was murdered so brutally, but how can we pretend that it is any less horrible than the killing of Iraqi prisoners of war, which we allegedly have done? That is convenient posturing of the worst sort, presuming that some human lives are more valuable than others, or that equally heinous crimes are permissible if the victim is one of "them." As Americans, do we believe that a life is worth less if that life held beliefs different from ours? It is shameful to deny prisoners the rights of the Geneva

Convention just because we disagree with their beliefs and positions. I am terrified that we are going to start rewriting the Constitution, once we start taking fundamental rights away from people based on differences of opinion. Please remember, we lose credibility with the rest of the world when we take these clearly self-serving positions. Wouldn't we gain far more by denying all violence against all prisoners unilaterally? Perhaps by the time you are president there won't be any violence against any prisoners in Iraq, in Guantánamo, in our own prisons in the U.S.A. If that's the case, maybe you could expand on this logic and apply it to some of your other problems.

Hopefully, Next Mr. President, you will not so automatically discount what a member of your opposing party is saying. The far left looking across at the far right, and both assuming they are lying, just isn't working. It's a waste of time. The only way we are ever going to fix anything is if we can get our disparate factions talking to one another. We all live in the same world, not in different ones. We need to face that fact. We all stand on the same ground. Let's share the ground. Common ground.

BOB BALABAN produced and costarred in *Gosford Park,* and he produced and directed the hit off-Broadway evening *The Exonerated.* Balaban has appeared in more than fifty movies, including *Midnight Cowboy, Absence of Malice,* and *A Mighty Wind.* Currently he is producing and directing a series for VH1 and the IFC.

Michele Lee

ELLIOTT FORREST

I would say this to any president: Don't be so dogmatic. Don't point so many fingers. Let's have fewer labels. It is time to reach across the aisle and support and respect the loyal opposition. Today, I see no spirit of compromise, no working together. Every issue seems bound for divisiveness; everything is politics, with a winner and a loser. I have a message for you, Mr. President: It is the American people who lose.

As I look at the newspapers and the newsreels and the talk shows, it's hard to stay off the antidepressants! How do we live each day with such partisan antagonism running rampant? Meanwhile, problems go unsolved while the noise level, passing for debate, gets higher and higher.

Am I crazy, or do I remember a time when there was a more gentlemanly politics? When I was a kid, you didn't see all the mudslinging that appears on the campaign ads and the spewing from the spin doctors. You can hardly understand an issue today with all that partisan posturing! Is that the point, to keep us from understanding?

But I don't want this opportunity to pass without making a few wishes. I don't have the answers, mind you, but I just want to say what it is I think we *should* have, what we deserve. Our kids are in deep trouble. They are not getting the emotional, physical, and parental support they need to thrive as future citizens. Every child should go to preschool; every child should go off to school in the morning healthy and well fed, ready to learn, because that is the only way they are going to be able to contribute to society, with college as their path, not prison. We have taken arts out of the schools to a great extent. This is undermining the fabric of our society. The arts help develop the spiritual self, and this is as important as acquiring math and science skills. We must have a society that makes music and poetry a part of its identity, how it sees itself, and this must begin at school.

Of course these simple requests can inspire a firestorm of debate as to how it can be done, who should pay, whether the government should be involved, and on and on. That's inevitable. But let's agree that these are worthy goals, and let's agree to disagree about how best to achieve them, but not to stop talking and listening, to work and work till we reach a solution.

Mr. President, let's drop the dogma. Let's find a way to build a stronger, healthier America. Let the world see us doing that in a spirit of mutual, respectful cooperation. That would be a great American message.

MICHELE LEE, actress, producer, and director, is known worldwide for her Emmy-nominated role as Karen in the landmark CBS series *Knots Landing.* She was discovered in Broadway's *How to Succeed in Business Without Really Trying,* in a role that she later repeated on-screen. Then, in 1970 she found herself in Disney's hit classic *The Love Bug.* In 1996 Lee became the first woman to produce, direct, write, and star in a film for television. She has won Tony nominations for the Broadway musical *Seesaw* and most recently for *The Allergist's Wife.*

Jerry Stiller

TONY ESPARZA/CBS

Mr. President, among the many things that are on my mind . . .

There are so many issues dealing with the world situation right now, but I think the most important is to find a way to get out of Iraq so that lives will not be wasted.

I don't know the answer as to how. But it seems to me that this situation has to be resolved by the people in that region. Our job is to facilitate bringing these people together and then remove ourselves as objects of scorn and hate. We have become the problem. We removed one only to become one. It is time to leave.

On the domestic front, I would urge you to let medical research advance the way the medical community wishes, with increased stem-cell work. We cannot stand in the way of doctors and researchers who see vast possibilities in stem-cell applications. In fact, we should help fund the research. Precious time is being lost, lives being wasted, as we allow a philosophical-religious debate to stand in the way of progress. Being seventy-seven years old, I am very well aware of how the body at a certain point starts to feel the effects of aging. It's like a car that's been running since the day you bought it, and believe me, you can't trade it in. I checked. I am a grandparent. I am also a son who had a dad who lived to see a hundred years. I know the burden that a deteriorating quality of life can put on the next generation. The surviving children endure the pain, the responsibilities, the financial burden of an aging population that could be greatly helped by stem-cell research. Don't stand in the way. Over time this will erode our country's ability to prosper. Money that could be used to invest and help our country remain vital is instead poured into long-term care facilities. We need research, help, hope. I ask for your leadership on this and many issues.

Thank you.

JERRY STILLER is one-half of the comedy team Stiller and Meara. He was nominated for an Emmy for his role as the curmudgeonly father Frank Costanza on *Seinfeld* and now costars on *The King of Queens.* His theater credits include *Hurlyburly, The Ritz, The Golden Apple,* and *What's Wrong with This Picture?* Films include *The Taking of Pelham 1-2-3, Hairspray,* and *Zoolander.*

Minnie  Driver

SASHA GUSOV/WWW.SASHAGUSOV.COM

Dear El Jefe: Of the five core issues I would love to spend all day discussing with you (trade, health-care reform, education, the environment, and the war in Iraq) I have chosen trade because of its far-reaching power to alter the socioeconomic (im)balance of our world, and because everyone else is going to be talking about the other things.

I needn't tell you how many causes of death in our world seem impossible to prevent; however, I feel it imperative to remind you that poverty is not one of them.

Economic growth is powered by international trade, and it is the surest way of saving lives, globally, that exists today (I have a feeling that you very much want to interject right now about your commitment to poverty reduction in the Third World; with all due respect, I wish you wouldn't . . . thank you). I am going to say this next thing very passionately and loudly as if at a demonstration:

TRADE RULES ARE RIGGED! (repeat 3×)

The rules that govern trade are rigged mightily in favor of the First World (the U.S. and the EU). There is also an arsenal of double standards to back this up. The World Trade Organization (WTO) apparently offers an opportunity for fair trade, but it turns out this "fairness" is not available to developing countries. Why? Why, when poor countries export to rich-country markets, do they face tariff barriers that are four times higher than those rich countries pay? These barriers cost them $100 billion a year—*twice as much as they receive in aid!* The inequity compounds further if one takes a moment to remember that if Africa, East Asia, South Asia, and Latin America were to increase their share of world exports by just 1 percent, the resulting gains in income would lift 128 million people out of poverty. I know, it probably just slipped your mind. . . . In Africa alone, this would generate *$70 billion!!!* Approximately five times the amount that continent receives in aid. Wouldn't $70 billion be a load off your mind, not to mention the budget?

Now, I need to tell you I understand the political significance of behemoth-type transnational companies to the governments of the First World, but it's indefensible that they have been left free to engage in any sort of deplorable investment and employment practices with only timid, "voluntary guidelines" to constrain them.

You blame the WTO and they blame you.

This is not good enough. There is vicious global bullying going on, by transnational corporations, by the

World Bank, and by the International Monetary Fund. Our countries keep their markets closed (remember: *Trade rules are rigged!*) while poor countries are strong-armed into opening theirs at breakneck speed, often with damaging consequences to their communities.

The international trading system is not something that is by nature out of control; it is a system of exchange whose rules reflect political choices. I am asking you, Mr. President, as a leader of the free world, to choose. . . .

- Choose to create a new model of inclusive globalization.
- Choose to create more of a balance between the weak and vulnerable and the rich and powerful.

However naive it sounds, please factor the lives of millions and millions of people with no voice into the unstoppable dictates of economic growth. Please champion them.

Thank you for your time.

MINNIE DRIVER is a British actress who lives and works predominantly in the United States. She is active on behalf of women's labor rights in developing countries, and would very much like you to consider the T-shirt you are wearing and the conditions under which it was made.

DONALD MCPHERSON

Matthew
Modine

Well, hello, Mr. President. It's such a pleasure to make your acquaintance.

Oh, thank you. Thank you very much. Um, uh, you seem to be having trouble sitting up straight in your chair. Here, let me help you. . . .

Wow! Sweet Jesus! You seem to be missing something. Something important. Holy Christ! Where's your spine, Mr. President?!!

What's that? It was part of the price? The price you had to pay? Oh, I see. Yes. Yes, of course, life is full of compromises. Yes. Yes. Special-interest groups. Foreign policies. Paybacks. Yes, but your spine?

So, your spine was the price you had to pay in order to become the leader of this powerful nation? No? Not the full price? Only a part? Jeez. What else would you have to give up? I mean, I don't want to sound rude, but look at yourself. You're like an eel.

I don't understand, Mr. President. How can not having backbone . . . sorry, a spine, be advantageous for our country's most powerful leader?

You don't have to take a stand? You don't have to stand up for what you believe in? But, technically, that's the job.

Well, yes, technically, you can't stand up. So, right. You don't have to. Right. Not without being propped up by those people you gave your spine to. I don't know if I could give up my spine, Mr. President. It's a huge price to pay. What's that . . . ?

Your spine was just the deposit? Like, sort of a down payment, so to speak? Your will? You had to give them your will!

And your soul! Good grief.

But, why? What are you left with? To gain the world, but lose your soul! What does this all say about democracy in the free world!

There is no democracy? But . . . it's been replaced? Ever since the end of the Cold War . . . *Finito?* But that's what America is fighting for! That's what we're always fighting for! Democracy! A square meal and a color TV in everyone's home!

Democracy is just a word we throw around to justify a war? That's horrible, Mr. President. Please don't say things like that. People are dying. Young Americans are fighting for that word. Please don't say they aren't dying for . . .

What? Democracy is dead? Stop grinning at me, Mr. President. You're scaring me. We live in a democracy, remember! No, no, I won't stop saying it! Why!?

You want to what? Whisper in my ear? But . . . okay, all right. What is it?

Capitalism? What about it?

No Republican Party?

No Democratic Party?

There are no more parties?

No more borders? But . . . but . . . only capitalism?

Just capitalism now? Wow.

MATTHEW MODINE has more than four dozen film credits to his name, including starring roles in *Full Metal Jacket, Birdy, Gross Anatomy, Married to the Mob, Memphis Belle,* and *Any Given Sunday.*

Harry
Shearer

Hello, Mr. (or Ms.) President: No one knows better than you that the most profound corrupting influence on your ability to govern responsively (and responsibly) is the insatiable need to raise, by any means necessary (and some even legal) the funds required to maintain the ever-increasing volume of media advertising that characterizes the modern political campaign. And no one knows better than you that one of the most powerful lobbies in Washington, the media industry, stands athwart any attempt to change this system, since it benefits them so richly and regularly. As the value of other advertising is doubted and debated, the biennial shower of political campaign expenditures becomes a more and more impor-tant part of the media owners' revenue stream.

Therefore I suggest that you resist the pressure to embark on any more piecemeal "reforms" of the cam-paign funding process (which only encourages the lawyers of your and your opponents' national committees to find cleverer work-arounds). Instead, I would urge you to try to bring the United States into conformity with every other Western industrial democracy, and push for a bill that would require, as a condition of the broadcast license, that each licensee devote a specified amount of time to free, half-hour campaign broadcasts by any parties whose candidates are deemed eligible for national debates. The broadcasters will scream and squeal about the First Amendment, and your job will be to remind them, cheerfully but frequently, that they operate on the public airwaves, according to the Communications Act, in the public interest, convenience, and necessity.

It will be a tough job, but how would you rather spend your time—trying to push such a meaningful reform through a recalcitrant Congress, or spending most of your second and fourth years in office attending fundraisers? It's your choice.

One more thing: Do you validate parking?

HARRY SHEARER is perhaps best known for his work as cocreator and costar in the mockumentary *This Is Spinal Tap,* in which he portrayed heavy-metal rocker Derek Smalls. His politically oriented radio show, *Le Show,* is in its twenty-first year of nationwide broadcast. For more than a decade he has lent his voice to various characters on *The Simpsons.* Shearer most recently appeared as the transgender bass player Mark/Marta Shubb in *A Mighty Wind.*

Margaret Carlson

Mr. President: Let me invoke the late Tip O'Neill's oft-quoted chestnut, "All politics is local," and add this finer point, "and personal." For this drive-by meeting, sir, I would like to have by my side Michael J. Fox and Christopher Reeve, as well as my best friend and brother, all of whose lives would be improved, if not saved, if you would rethink your illogical decisions on stem-cell research, a field of inquiry that holds out hope for curing Alzheimer's, Parkinson's, spinal injuries, diabetes, and a host of other diseases.

Other than the war in Iraq, no recent presidential decision has cost more lives than the Bush administration's ruling severely restricting the research using stem cells. The White House went to such lengths to dramatize the chief executive's agonizing over this. Oh, the books he read. Oh, the time he spent away from clearing brush and working out to study bioethics. Yet he might as well have spent the time playing video golf for all the reason he brought to it. In the president's long-awaited announcement in August 2001, he bowed deeply to the pro-lifers in his party and decided that no new stem-cell lines could be created, concluding that to do otherwise would involve taxpayer dollars in the creation and destruction of embryos. The president said not to worry, however, enough tissue—sixty-four lines—already existed.

But the president was wrong on the facts and illogical in his conclusion, and both things have devastated the research community. Nineteen—not sixty-four—stem-cell lines are available; not enough. And federally funded scientists look in frustration at new stem-cell lines created from discarded embryos abroad. They can't touch them.

By the president's own logic (or lack of it), stem-cell research immediately could be vastly expanded—and without creating or killing any new embryos. In vitro fertilization creates embryos by the hundreds of thousands, which are NOW sitting on the shelves of fertility clinics of America, eventually to be discarded. There's no rational reason for not using them. Looked at through Bush's prism, researchers would be saving those embryos and saving life, in both senses of the phrase. To that end, 206 members of Congress, including three dozen pro-lifers, have signed a letter urging a presidential change of mind.

Mr. President, you can't rationally conclude that a five-day-old clump of cells, already existing as surplus material from IVF procedures, awaiting the trash bin, is as valuable as the life of a paralyzed teenager, or Michael J. Fox, who could stand in during our cameo meeting for the thousands of nameless and voiceless others watching years of their lives go by as an unsound argument derails the progress of medical research. Unlike tax cuts, there are flesh-and-blood consequences to this flawed decision. Let's be on the side of life—improving it, extending it, and, yes, saving it.

MARGARET CARLSON is the author of *Time* magazine's "Public Eye" column. She also serves as a panelist on CNN's *Inside Politics* and *The Capital Gang.* She is the author of *Anyone Can Grow Up: How George Bush and I Made It to the White House,* a memoir of growing up in a small town in Pennsylvania.

Charles
Grodin

We have two million people in prison in America. That represents 25 percent of the world's prison population, but America represents 5 percent of the world's overall population.

We have too many people whose lives, unjustifiably, have been taken away from them.

Elaine Bartlett, a welfare mother of four small children, after being enticed by the prospect of $2,500 by a police informant, carried a packet of four ounces of cocaine to Albany, where she was arrested. She had sixteen years of her life taken away because of New York's Rockefeller drug laws. She had never been in trouble with the law before, and had five dollars in her pocket when she was arrested. The police wanted to build their arrest record, the informant wanted a break from the police for his own drug dealing, and nobody cared that a welfare mother, not a drug dealer, was entrapped. Her children were, and are, devastated.

In California, Brandon Hein is serving a life sentence with no chance of parole. He has the same sentence as Gary Ridgeway, who admitted to killing forty-eight women, but Brandon Hein didn't kill anyone. What did he do? He got drunk and got into a fight that involved six boys. One boy stabbed another, who bled to death. Brandon did nothing but get into a fight. He didn't kill anyone. He didn't steal anything. Most of the boys knew one another, and even though nothing was stolen, Brandon and others were convicted of *intended* robbery. The way the felony murder rule is applied in California put this eighteen-year-old (now twenty-seven) in prison for life with no chance to get out.

Elaine Bartlett and Brandon Hein are two examples of America's human rights violations. We say we go to war with countries because of how they treat their people, so we had better not be guilty of that kind of heinous behavior. Sadly, we are, not only obviously outside America, but in America.

I would ask that we take a hard look at what we sometimes do in America to our own people who come before our justice system because of too much mandatory sentencing and not enough wise judgment.

CHARLES GRODIN is an award-winning actor and writer. He has published five highly acclaimed books, was a commentator for *60 Minutes II,* and is currently a commentator for the CBS News Radio Network.

PHIL POYNTER

Bianca
Jagger

Mr. President, I would urge you, if indeed I am talking to President Bush, to reconsider your support for the death penalty. While you were governor of Texas, you presided over the executions of 152 prisoners on death row. You now have the opportunity to support a state-by-state moratorium on the death penalty and impose a moratorium on federal executions. Let's bring American justice in line with all the other industrialized nations of the world.

There are many practical reasons to abolish the death penalty: It is not a deterrent to violent crime, as study after study has shown; the U.S. violent crime rate remains higher than that of other countries that have banished the death penalty, including allies such as Canada, Germany, and England. Mr. President, the fear of a state-sponsored execution does not stop crime. Executions are costly: in

Texas, a death-penalty case costs an average of $2.3 million, about three times the cost of imprisoning someone at the highest security level for forty years. There is no basis for the argument that death is cheaper than a life sentence without parole. But even more alarming, the death penalty is too often unjustly served upon the innocent. More than one hundred prisoners facing execution have already been exonerated and their convictions over-turned. These innocent people were about to be killed by the state and only the intervention of concerned groups and attorneys providing the kind of legal aid they had no access to in their original trials spared them. Even more outrageous, Mr. President, is that in America, while juve-niles under eighteen cannot drink, vote, or serve in the military, they can be executed, in flagrant violation of international law. Mr. President, this is simply an intoler-able solution. I urge you to shift your government's focus away from execution and instead to work toward the pre-vention and treatment of sexual, physical, and emotional abuse of children in order to prevent them from suc-cumbing to a life of crime.

Mr. President, those are the practical reasons for sus-pending the death penalty, reasons that are compelling enough to inspire many people who otherwise believe in eye-for-an-eye justice to oppose it. But there's another, more philosophical reason, one that gets at the nature of human beings and the proper role of government. I ask you, as the person who holds the most powerful position in America, one who often invokes the sanctity of life and who has taken the moral high ground on numerous issues—Mr. President, is the death penalty ever just? Is a society truly operating at its highest moral level when its only solution to prevent violent crimes is to kill? Are we not a bankrupt society when we do not allow the possibility for change, rehabilitation, and redemption? During your tenure as governor, I witnessed Gary Graham's execution. Across America and throughout the world people believe Graham was innocent of the crime for which he was executed. I felt ashamed to be a member of a society that was sponsoring a state-sanctioned killing of an innocent man. Mr. President, if you truly believe in the sanctity of life, please support a moratorium on the death penalty.

BIANCA JAGGER has campaigned for human rights, social and economic justice, and environmental protection throughout the world for more than twenty years. Since the mid-1990s, she has worked with Amnesty International and other organizations to abolish the death penalty.

FADIL BERISHA

Joe
Piscopo

I implore you to put as much effort into rebuilding our inner cities here in America as we do in every other part of the world.

It is inexcusable that we discount the problems of our cities—which affect us all in some way—but are so preoccupied with civilizations in other parts of the world. Granted, if they need us, the United States will always and should always be there. But let's look down Main Street USA first!

Help our cities!

If we, as a country, would create product-manufacturing bases in cities like Camden, New Jersey, or South Central, L.A., it would create jobs, respect, and a true sense of community.

I suggest a "corporate summit"' with Wall Street icons and union leaders to discuss ways to make "Made in

America" a more common sight. Make those Nikes on the "less fortunate" side of Houston. Make those celebrity clothes in Newark.

I know that this would take an effort by the CEOs of our major corporations to take fewer bonuses (sure, they'd have to settle for Learjets and sell off those G-5s). Also, the unions (I am an ardent member of several) might help in a big way with some concessions to combat overseas slave labor.

In short, Mr. President, we are long overdue to first reach out to those less fortunate right here at home.

JOE PISCOPO is an actor, comedian, and former star of *Saturday Night Live.* He is also the founder of the Positive Impact Foundation, a nonprofit organization highlighting the many positive images of at-risk youth in America.

THE CREATIVE COALITION ARCHIVES

Richard Lewis

Mr. President, I beg of you, don't feel the need whatsoever to laugh, perhaps get melancholy, or even break down for that matter in response to anything that I might have the courage to ask you in this surreal opportunity that you have given me to ask you a few questions before your scheduled ten thousand briefings prior to your photo ops and usual screening of *Dr. Strangelove.*

For what it's worth, I've been to the Oval Office before, as a guest of President Clinton. However, back then I wasn't a sober man who thankfully is coming up on a decade of sobriety, nor was I sadly, tremendously middle-aged, as I am now, and to be frank, crazily curious about what makes someone like yourself, who has a job that I believe is almost as hard as making a living as a comedian. Moreover, the consequences of your daily actions are obviously closer in reality to what Jackson

Browne once wrote when he sang the words "lives in the balance" than little old me just hopefully getting laughs on stage and possibly being rebooked and not ripped off again by unprincipled promoters. I'll concede that although my job is oftentimes more difficult than yours and the only focus group I have is the audience, even if I bomb, it's not the end of the world and pardon the poor use of the language but if you bomb, it might be. It's the latter which brings me to my reason for being here.

I simply want to ask you a few questions. I don't expect you to reply spontaneously or down the line respond to me with a missive, although should I be so lucky, I'd love to have it on White House stationery in order to impress the improbable woman of my dreams and maybe get lucky sexually.

Was that a chuckle, Mr. President? Oh, then it must be the rumblings I hear in the outer hall by the Secret Service, which no doubt is signaling that my time here is coming down to the wire. That said, I've just decided that even though I've gone sleepless for nights making lists of literally hundreds of potential, burning queries I had for someone in your position, I think I can boil it down to just a few questions. One, why can't the leader of the United States of America try to comprehend that most of the world has, rightfully, their own belief systems, mostly alien to ours, or just understandably being so poor or living under some scumbag dictator suffer from "USA envy" and that, in most cases, trying to win their hearts and minds over in lieu of taking care of our very own poor and suffering population, at the very least simultaneously, is perhaps the single, most misguided approach to governing in modern history? And lastly, and I pray you don't take this the wrong way.

Trust me, sir, I mean well, and may God be with you. And if I may, I hope God knows when to help you privately and when he can chill and just let the country govern itself. Oops! I got political. Oh, hell, I'm only human and that's my biggest flaw.

I know, I know, I have to go. All right, here goes. And I pray you don't get mad. My most pressing probe is whether you honestly think upon becoming the president of the United States, that for you, and those who preceded you, it is merely just a way, in some gargantuan, temporary lapse of sanity that had nothing to do with politics, love, vision, passion or goodwill for the "people," but rather tragically, some simpleminded, narcissistic notion that you could, after having been elected, go to bed every night rationalizing that you have the biggest penis in the world? Love to the first lady. Ciao.

RICHARD LEWIS, actor, comedian, and author, has taken his lifelong therapy fodder and carved it into a commanding art form. With critically acclaimed appearances on HBO's *Curb Your Enthusiasm,* he is charted in *GQ's* "20th Century's Most Influential Humorists."

Caroline
Rhea

COURTESY OF WARNER BROS.

Dear Mr. President:

Depending on who you are, you may have a lot of 'splainin' to do . . . but never mind.

What is your favorite amendment, and why? I'm guessing it's not the first, since you tried to get rid of it.

I'd like to say I love your dress, who's your designer, but this is probably not the year. So let me ask, Who do you really think the tax cut is going to help? And how many of them do you know personally? Do you really truly think it is going to help the poor? How many of them do you know personally?

What was the capital of the state you were govenor of?

Did you read *Hamlet* in high school and did it have a deeply profound effect on you?

Would you ever call in sick one day and have the vice president run the country, or has that already happened?

How can you consider us to be the richest country in the world if we don't have socialized medicine?

How indebted do you feel to the groups who have given vast sums to your campaign? Is Halliburton the only company you are going to name a country after?

Is your ego a weapon of mass destruction?

Do you feel that a woman has a right to decide when a man should or should not have a vasectomy?

Have you ever won at Scrabble? Tic-tac-toe?

If you believe that every American has the right to life, liberty, and the pursuit of happiness, how can you be against stem-cell research?

Do you think that the first lady is entitled to have a political opinion? A political opinion that is different from yours?

Which actor do you feel has portrayed the president in the way you would like to be portrayed—Michael Douglas, Martin Sheen, Gary Sinise, Edward Hermann, William Devane, Darth Vader?

Do you think it is ever effective to run the country based on fear . . . ? Roosevelt didn't, Kennedy didn't, Johnson wouldn't . . .

Would you ever let Michael Moore interview you?

Do you know who Michael Moore is? What about Demi Moore? Do you think Ashton is too young for her?

I'm not done. I could be asking you how do you sleep at night, or how do you relax?

Do you think anyone's private life should be the business of anyone else?

Okay, maybe I don't care if you disagree with your wife.

Yes, I do.

CAROLINE RHEA is a stand-up comedienne and actress who believes in democracy.

Sean 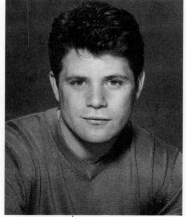 Astin

HARRY LANGDON/WWW.HARRYLANGDON.COM

In the spring of 2004 I traveled with my wife and two daughters to Shanghai, China. I had already learned a bit about Chinese culture when I was studying history and English at UCLA, and I'd been to China before. But on this trip, as a father and a person interested in making films in China, my eyes were wide open. I was able to experience firsthand the beauty of a civilization that has survived for thousands of years. The question I would put to the future president is this: Considering how young our country is in the history of the world, have you thought about the lasting impact that your administration will have on global civilization over the next few hundred years?

When I wonder about what issues will have the greatest long-term impact on the world, I think first of EDUCATION!!!

There is extraordinary human capital in our country. While I am loath to use such a coarse monetary term to refer to our beloved citizens, I believe that our people must be better educated, nurtured, and inspired! For my money, education is the most important investment our society can make in terms of our future. It seems obvious to me that our nation has a responsibility to inform the citizenry of what has gone before and what is likely to happen in the near and far future. We should be teaching everyone how to think creatively and independently. People are our richest resource. I'm worried that as we try to protect ourselves from those who would do us harm, and allocate monies to do so, we are not investing enough in the education of our children.

I'm not sure how much of this is a federal issue that the president can actually impact, but surely the chief executive has an enormous leadership position with the implied responsibility to ensure that our country continues to evolve.

I would encourage the president to remember that he (Kerry or Bush) can have a manifest impact on governments at every level. I'd want to study the president's comments so that I could sense for myself how genuinely passionate and knowledgeable he is. I'd want to know precisely what significant changes he was working on to affect the quality of public school education.

In both the arms race and the space race, Cold War America responded with determination. In my estimation and hopefully in the future president's, the moment to engage in a global education race is upon us. A race toward knowledge based on developing skills for self-expression is required in order for us to coexist peacefully with all the peoples of the world!

Specifically, I am very worried about the forty-four million illiterate adults in America.

I'm excited about working with whoever is my president on these and many other important issues!

While my family was in Shanghai, we spent four hours at the Shanghai museum, marveling at how elegantly that country's thousands of years of culture were presented.

The president and all of us should be thinking about our far future. All Americans would do well to think about how their lives and work will contribute to the presentation of our culture.

SEAN ASTIN is an actor-director and social and political activist. Among his numerous film credits are starring roles in the award-winning *Lord of the Rings* series, the acclaimed *Rudy*, and *The Goonies*. He also received an Academy Award nomination for his short film *Kangaroo Court*, which he coproduced. He recently took an oath of office with the White House chief of staff to serve on the President's Council on Services and Civic Participation; he has also served as a civilian aide to the secretary of the army since 1995 and serves on the board of the National Center for Family Literacy. Astin is a member of The Creative Coalition's board of directors.

Peter
Coyote

Dear Mr. President: When did our electricity become intermittent; our schools, bridges, and roads fall into disrepair; our high school sports teams get canceled; and the integrity of our voting become questionable? In the last twenty years, according to the Government Accounting Office, income for 90 percent of American workers rose $2,700, or five cents an hour. Income for the super-wealthy—one-half of 1 percent of the population—rose on average $24 million, even as their taxes fell.

This nearly universal degradation is directly attributable to America's global ambitions and the military expenditures required to defend them. The current military budget dwarfs the sums spent on health care, K-12 education, or research and development. *Whose* interests are being served and/or protected by these military expenditures?

Mr. President, you have the opportunity to use your bully pulpit and accomplish two critically important things. One would be to change the way elections are financed in this country. The corporate sector has overwhelmed the civic sector and skewed budgeting priorities. One cannot have a civil society without public schools, libraries, neighborhood organizations, and public health and civic organizations, and yet they are being starved out of existence. Until federal elections are publicly financed, until free airtime for qualified candidates and debates on every network are requirements for FCC licensing, the needs and concerns of ordinary citizens will never be reflected in public policy.

The other critical thing you might do would be to explain clearly and cogently to the American people that *the economy is a subset of the environment and not the other way around.* It is impossible to have a healthy economy in a sick environment. We can no longer eat tuna and swordfish safely. The water in hundreds of American cities is poisoned with lead and mercury. Correcting dilemmas like this will require time spans greater than the next election cycle. In order to support such an effort, our people need to be informed.

You might initiate a domestic Marshall Plan to "rebuild our national wealth." Our nation could employ the same loggers and machinery currently ravaging our forests to replant them and clean and repair salmon streams. The same procedure could hold true for ranching, coal mining, and a host of destructive industries. Base our economy on the detoxifying and rebuilding of our national treasure, putting our labor force back to work in the process.

To accomplish this, you would have to take the lead in reversing the corporate-sponsored ideology about small government. You would need to explain that *only* government has the responsibility to see to the needs of the entire nation and not simply the corporate sector. You would have to reacquaint our people with the virtues of responsive government. The promise of the United States remains unfulfilled, Mr. President. What could be a more stirring, more redemptive legacy than keeping our word to history?

PETER COYOTE has acted in more than ninety feature films and television productions, including *E.T.*, *Jagged Edge*, and *Erin Brockovich*. He is also well known for his voice-over work, and has done numerous documentaries and television specials, including the Emmy Award–winning series *The Pacific Century*. In 1967, Coyote cofounded a political group known as The Diggers, an anarchistic group that supplied free food, housing, and medical aid to runaways in Haight-Ashbury. In 1998 he published a memoir, *Sleeping Where I Fall*, a chapter of which won the Pushcart Prize for writing excellence.

Montel
Williams

JEFF KATZ/PARAMOUNT

Mr. President: In the eyes of the public, I am an all-American tough guy, a former naval intelligence officer, a motivational speaker, and a TV talk-show host. I am beamed into the homes of millions of people around the globe each weekday. I urge individuals and family members to do better, to *be* better. But there is another side to my story.

For more than twenty years I have lived with a chronic, potentially debilitating disease called multiple sclerosis (MS). I have neuralgic pain in my feet and legs so severe that I have twice attempted suicide—the ultimate trauma to my kids and family, the ultimate sin against God. I have stayed awake for nights on end, rocked by violent spasms in my legs. Physicians have prescribed myriad painkillers and antispasmodic drugs—each more toxic than the next, each less effective than the other. I have taken Percocet, Vicodin, OxyContin, and a morphine drip, risking overdose to subdue the pain. Instead, I became spacey and dull. I could not function. Something had to give. Something did. I discovered medical marijuana, which is illegal everywhere in the country, according to federal law, even though eight states have laws in effect that allow patients to use it without fear of arrest.

On many days, I live with pain that is a seven on a scale of one to ten, and with nerves so raw that if you brush against me in an elevator, I just want to scream. Medical marijuana brings that pain down to a three or four. But every day I am forced to make the choice between criminality and management of my symptoms.

Mr. President, I am not alone. Tens of thousands of Americans, your citizens, make this daily choice. They are people like me who suffer from pain and spasms from MS, wasting from AIDS and cancer, and from numerous other symptoms. Because of medical marijuana, those of us with chronic or life-threatening illnesses have emerged from the haze of narcotic-based or morphinelike painkillers and other toxic medications to continue being productive citizens.

For people like me who have been through the gamut of FDA-approved drugs with no relief, marijuana has given us our lives back. It allows us to sleep through the night, to gain weight and strength, to read a bedtime story to our child, to run an office. It offers us the liberty—the freedom to live with dignity—that is one of our inalienable rights as American citizens.

The states with strong medical marijuana laws have built-in safety measures to ensure that the drug is not opened up to recreational users. It must be recommended by a physician, and, in most cases, patients must register with a state or local health authority. There are also reasonable limits on how much of the drug an individual or a caretaker can possess.

Mr. President, I urge you to support legal access to medical marijuana across our great nation. I urge you to support legislation that would change marijuana from a Schedule I drug, a group that includes heroin, LSD, and Quaaludes, to a Schedule II drug, which includes drugs, like amphetamines and morphine, that are prescribed in extreme cases. As a Schedule II drug, marijuana could be prescribed by a physician—with all the checks and balances to keep patients like me safe.

That's all I ask of you. True compassion with all the conservative medical and legal boundaries in place. What better legacy to leave?

MONTEL WILLIAMS, an Emmy Award–winning talk-show host, has completed thirteen seasons of the nationally syndicated *The Montel Williams Show.* He is a retired decorated naval officer, a motivational speaker, and the author of six books, including *Climbing Higher,* on living with MS. He is also a member of The Creative Coalition's advisory board.

Tom  Fontana

SIMKO

Mr. President, I don't want to talk about education, the underclass, health care, the environment, jobs, the national debt, foreign policy, judicial appointments, capital punishment, media consolidation, funding for the arts, stem-cell research, abortion, or any of the other seismic issues facing the United States during the course of your term.

I don't want to talk about your military record, your religious affiliation, or your sexual appetites. That'll be too distracting.

And let's not talk about the latest opinion polls or how to work with Congress.

Okay, I really want to find out if you've ever watched *Oz,* but . . .

First and foremost, I want to ask you a series of questions. Do you think, in the name of homeland security, that we have permanently damaged the Bill of Rights? In the fervor of patriotism, have we been mistreating innocent aliens, immigrants, or our own citizens? In the all-or-nothing war against terrorism, have we sanctioned torture?

Mr. President, since America is not the first country in the history of mankind ever to be attacked, how long do we get to be high-minded and arrogant toward other nations? How many times are we allowed to justify our actions by evoking the memories of dead firefighters?

When does righteous anger become blind vengeance? At what point does fear become a stronger motivating force than reason? When does the warranty on our moral superiority run out? And are you, Mr. President, the only one who gets to decide?

Take your time answering. When you are done, if there's a few minutes left, we can discuss *Oz*—the HBO show, sir, not the movie. Though I'll bet you know a thing or two about the man behind the curtain.

TOM FONTANA is the executive producer and creator of HBO's first hour-long drama and Cable Ace Award–winning series *Oz*. He was also the executive producer of, and a writer on, the long-running and critically acclaimed NBC series *Homicide: Life on the Street.* During the show's seven-year run, he won an Emmy Award, two Writers' Guild Awards, three Peabody Awards, and four Television Critics Awards. As a writer and producer for the television series *St. Elsewhere,* Fontana was awarded two Emmy Awards, a Peabody Award, and a Writers' Guild Award. He wrote the ABC special *The Fourth Wiseman* and was the executive producer of *American Tragedy* for CBS and *Shot in the Heart* for HBO Films. Fontana is a member of The Creative Coalition.

KIRSTEN GETCHELL

Kathleen
York

Good morning, President Kerry (hope springs eternal):

I'd like to start off by thanking you for being noble enough, or insane enough, to accept the job as leader of a superpower nation. It certainly is not an occupation many of us would be willing to take on (seeing how constant, continual stress is commonly thought of as "No Fun"). Five minutes isn't nearly enough time to discuss everything about the governance of this country that inspires and weighs on me, so I will limit myself to some basics.

Air quality: Half of harmful ground-level ozone is caused by combustion engine vehicles. Can we (finally) create legislation to force the automobile industry to transition toward the nonpolluting alternative energy sources that have existed for years?

Food quality: I ask you to read the independent studies done on irradiated and genetically modified foods. I believe that enough information has been gathered to consider the danger they impose on the human body and our food supply at large.

Other pet peeves: the injection of hormones into livestock and the continued use of known carcinogenic chemical fertilizers and preservatives. Outside of an absolute ban on certain chemicals used in farming, I believe growers and distributors should be made to put a list of the pesticides and residual chemical fertilizers (that remain on the produce even after washing) alongside their products at the supermarket. I believe consumers should be able to make choices regarding the content of the produce they are eating.

Community and education: I would LOVE to see non-violent conflict resolution taught in our public schools right alongside English, math, history, and science.

Foreign affairs: I implore you to do everything you can to put an end to our subversive meddling in foreign governments in the name of U.S. corporate interests. If we have any hope of inspiring trust from the rest of the world, our soulless "profit at any price" behavior has got to stop. I fear that we are fast becoming an island—a fat, wealthy island—in the sea of the world's hatred.

In the end, I believe that any decision that you, or any of us, will ever make can be profoundly impacted by a simple projection into the future. Twenty- or thirty-odd years from now, in the uncompromising silence of your deathbed when you reflect on your "time of influence," will you feel that you did everything in your power, regardless of partisanship, special-interest paybacks, criticism, or concerns of reelection, to make this world a kinder, healthier, and more just place? By your presence here on earth, are you making this place better than how you found it? Deep in our hearts, I believe this is the question we all must ask ourselves.

Are we willing to have less materially to have more in grace, in dignity? The future of countless generations rests on your (and all of our) shoulders. May we find the courage to be worthy of the position we have been given.

KATHLEEN YORK is an accomplished actress and singer-songwriter (known as Bird York), and now a budding screenwriter. Her music has been heard nationally on NPR as well as in numerous films and television shows. As an actress, she has been seen in a wide variety of television and film projects, most recently as Andrea Wyatt on NBC's *The West Wing*.

Giancarlo
Esposito

Mr. President: I want to talk to you for five minutes about the outsourcing of America, which has sent so many jobs overseas while Americans go without work and our manufacturing base erodes. Does a global economy mean Americans no longer have to work? Can we just get other countries to do our work for us? What are the long-term effects of this? Can it be good? I would say no.

America has changed with time, and will continue to do so as time goes forward. In this uncertain era, change has become even more profound as many Americans get richer and the world around them gets poorer.

I grew up in the turbulent 1960s, when America was struggling to define itself. Back then, pride in American-made products, goods, and services was at its height and it seemed that Americans *made* for America. Today it seems that about everything is "farmed out," "jobbed out," or contracted to someone or some place that can manufacture it cheaper, faster, and better than we can. But is it really cheaper if it costs us more later? Is it really better? What happens when you skip a generation of skilled laborers? What will happen to our all-important manufacturing base? What happens when we don't have the capacity to produce the products we use?

I ask you, Mr. President, to reinvigorate America by ending the overall outsourcing of American jobs and finding new creative ways to teach Americans how to make things cost-effectively once again and at living wages. My hope is that once again as a country we could learn to take pride in the label MADE IN AMERICA.

GIANCARLO ESPOSITO has appeared in more than fifty films and in numerous television movies and series. Recent film work includes *Ali, Piñero,* and *Waiting to Exhale.* He won two Obies for his roles in the off-Broadway productions *Distant Fires* and *Zooman and the Sign.* Esposito is on The Creative Coalition's board of directors.

SYLVIE LANCRENON

Juliette Lewis

Children are our future artists, our future leaders. So why are more than eight million of them taking prescribed, mind-altering psychiatric drugs? Why is it that, despite a commitment to a "war on drugs," six million of these kids are prescribed cocainelike stimulants that are now selling as street drugs for five dollars a pill? And why is it that despite a 1995 International Narcotics Control Board warning to the American government about abusive risk of drugs like Ritalin, the number of stimulants prescribed to children has increased 700 percent? Not to mention that children five years of age and younger are the fastest-growing segment of the nonadult population using antidepressants today.

Education is vital! Yet psychiatrists are allowed to preside over our classrooms, redefining educational problems as a mental "disorder" when there isn't a shred of scientific evidence to prove this. The kid has a chemical imbalance in his brain? Also not medically substantiated. Meanwhile, parents across the nation are coerced through schools into drugging their child, with threats of the child's expulsion or charges of medical neglect against the parents should they not quietly relinquish their rights. Let's get serious about education and take psychiatry and drugs out of the classroom. Let teachers do what they do best: teach. Let children do what they should do best: reach their full potential.

JULIETTE LEWIS garnered praise in 1991 from audiences and critics alike for her work alongside Robert De Niro, Nick Nolte, and Jessica Lange in Martin Scorsese's *Cape Fear*. She will soon be seen with Michael Madsen and Vincent Cassel in the independent feature *Blueberry*, and with Joshua Jackson and Donald Sutherland in *Aurora Borealis*.

CK
Lawford

ARUN NEVADER 2003

So I get five minutes with the next leader of the most powerful and disliked country on the planet. That would either be the great liberator wannabe or a Skull and Bones version of Elmer Gantry, unless a dirty bomb renders the whole thing moot. I'm thrilled. Five minutes to plead, rant, or lament the state of the world. Sorry, not nearly enough time! So, what's the point? Not to influence, certainly; by the time these guys make it to the Oval Office they're fully cooked political animals, in rigid lockstep with their ideology and special interest—any wiggle that's left serves political expediency and the quest for more power. Five minutes wouldn't make a dent. It might make me feel good showing the most powerful man in the world and my fans how much I care, but we're critical here and there isn't time for expending energy on ego gratification. I'll save my breath on Iraq, terror, the environment, and the erosion of civil liberties and get down to what inquiring minds really want to know.

What I'd really like is five minutes with Clinton. At least he was interesting and I might get details on the cigar.

"What's the thrill, Bill?" I love cigars and women and I've never thought of putting the two together like that. What am I missing here? Did he actually smoke the cigar, and if he did, how did it taste? I'm sure I'm not the only well-informed American who's interested in the effects of love juice on the wrapping of a good cigar. What kind of a cigar was it? Was it a Cuban? If it was, that's troubling on two fronts. It's fiscally irresponsible to use a pricey Cuban cigar in such a way and they're illegal. Maybe Ken Starr would have had better luck if instead of looking for a smoking gun he had looked for a smoking cigar. Does Clinton think he might have had more time to figure out what Al Qaeda was planning in those Afghan caves if he didn't have to explain his preoccupation with the nooks and crannies of White House interns?

Hey, I'd even take Nixon, but he's dead. Do you know that Nixon and Clinton are the only two U.S. presidents whose full names contain all the letters from the word *criminal*? That's interesting; I'd like to know what they think about that.

If Bush wins I've got a problem. It's obvious he doesn't give a rat's ass what anyone thinks except God. Wait a minute; I'd like to know what God sounds like. Does God speak to Bush through other people, and if he does, is His voice the same when Cheney is speaking and when Rummy is speaking? Does God talk to Bush all the time or just when he's wondering what to do about the evildoers?

I'd also like to chat about the breathtaking pyrotechnics of Shock & Awe. What did he think was more offensive, the images we weren't allowed to see of the results of that beautiful bombardment of Baghdad or seeing Janet Jackson's breast on the Super Bowl halftime show? Did he get to see those images on the ground?

Did he see Janet's breast? Which was more shocking? Did he turn away or TiVo it? What did Laura think? From there I would seamlessly segue into the subject of alcoholism and ask the president if "having had a problem with alcohol" he now thinks he's cured? Did he ever go to meetings? Does he turn his will and life over to a power greater than himself like they do in twelve-step programs or does he believe there is no power greater than himself and, like most untreated alcoholics, believe that he is the center of the universe and is hell-bent on imposing his will on the rest of the world? I might need more than five minutes if Bush wins.

If John Kerry wins I'd want to know why, having worked and lived in Washington for seventeen years, he'd want the job? Why, after marrying all the money, he needs all the power? Couldn't he do more harm or good in the private sector with all those dollars? Dick Cheney and friends need the Oval Office to get rich, but Kerry's already got the cash. So what's up, John? It couldn't have anything to do with seeking a newer world, or could it?

CK LAWFORD is an actor and producer who has appeared in such films as *Thirteen Days, Chump Change, Terminator 3, The Doors,* and *Russia House.*

Amanda Plummer

Mr. Next President: Of the many voices you hear from day to day, I wonder how often you hear the voice of our youth. So I am going to turn my time over to a young man who represents the future of this country. His name is Tristan Migliore, and he's a sixteen-year-old high school student from New Paltz, New York.

Mr. President, you come into power at a skewed time for our country. Our troops have been deployed illegitimately and are dying every day. We are fighting a war we cannot win, but I'm sure you know that already. Instead of talking about the war, then, I will take my opportunity here to speak to you about something that strikes me as just as important, something that will affect everyone on this planet, and is a

135

burden my generation is particularly concerned about: pollution.

I have two words for you, sir: Kyoto Protocol. Accepting the limitations set up by the United Nations in this document could save our planet and greatly reduce the burden of cleanup put on the shoulders of my generation. The world supply of petroleum is predicted to run out in fifty years and the U.S. reserves in twenty-five. While there will be no fuel left to burn, we will still be choking on the smog generated by our SUVs and power plants. The big businesses you are trying to support will boom for a moment, but in time our lungs will turn black and our ice caps will melt, things that will last much longer than those businesses.

Your administration denies the existence of global warming, yet you have instructed the military to construct a plan just in case such a thing does exist. To paraphrase something your predecessor said on a different topic, "It's the weather, stupid." (No insult intended.) From personal experience I can say global warming does exist; our winters are getting shorter and our summers hotter. And the future looks grim if we continue to cast a blind eye on one of the most important issues of our time.

In addition to your administration's rejection of the Kyoto Protocol, you also are working very dili- gently to get those pesky conservationists to let you drill for more oil in Alaska. The land that we control in Alaska is unique and should be respected, not pockmarked by oil drills and mines. The earth is a fragile place despite its mask of cold stone and ice. If we abuse it too much it will reflect the abuse directly back to us. The youth of today will suffer for your greed unless you start making changes.

Mr. President, action must be taken that is not simply in your own best interests but in the best interests of your fellow man. Please accept the restrictions that would be put in place by the Kyoto Protocol because they will help us survive. Our supply of oil is limited anyway; it is doomed to run out, so what is the point in scrambling over the last drops? If we move toward changing our energy systems into things like solar power and fuel cells, the transition can be easy and painless. There is still a chance for you to change the world for the better, and I am asking you to please start worrying about your planet and my future.

AMANDA PLUMMER is a Tony Award–winning actress who has appeared in more than eighty feature films, including Quentin Tarantino's critically acclaimed *Pulp Fiction* and Terry Gilliam's *The Fisher King.* Plummer won a Tony for her part in *Agnes of God,* and received Tony nominations for her roles in *Pygmalion* and *A Taste of Honey.* Her role in Showtime's *The Outer Limits* won her an Emmy Award for guest actress in a drama series.

Ms. Plummer's essay was written by Tristan Migliore, a junior at New Paltz High School. Migliore plans to study creative writing in college and is an avid music lover.

TRISTAN MIGLIORE is a sixteen-year-old junior at New Paltz (New York) High School. He plans to go to college for creative writing.

Eleanor  Clift

COURTESY OF *NEWSWEEK*

Mr. President, what troubles me most about our country is the caste system. If you've got money, you can buy your way out of the public-school system and send your children to private schools where they won't meet anybody different from themselves.

You can live in a gated community; you can drive an SUV, afford high parking rates, and vote against funding public transportation; and you can travel the information highway without fear of overcrowding from the masses. A recent study of students enrolled in the most selective colleges reveals the growing elitism, with high family income being the best predictor of who makes the cut. Yet there are vast sections of this country where a college degree is still a rarity, and where until the dawn of this century hardworking people could have a good life. With the loss first of manufacturing jobs and now many white-collar service jobs, too many good people worry about where they and their children fit into the new American workforce. There are too few jobs and too many unskilled people for this trend to have a happy ending unless you and your administration make the necessary investments in education. More testing is not the answer.

Providing the skills needed to survive in the global economy will require commitment from the top. For starters, I would urge you to lobby Congress to spring for the money to rebuild the crumbling infrastructure of public schools built in the 1960s when the Soviets launched Sputnik and we mobilized as a nation to meet the challenge of the space race. Terrorism is not the only threat to our way of life; equally troubling is our collective failure to address the growing disparity between the haves and the have-nots. The problem spills over into foreign policy, with too few of the elites having a direct stake in the war in Iraq. It's too easy to send young men and women to fight in a war that doesn't touch you or anybody in your social circle. What's missing when other people's children do the fighting for us is a shared sense of sacrifice. I believe that invading Iraq was a colossal misjudgment on the part of our leaders, and I would ask you, Mr. President, what is your plan to get the country on a more equal path and to restore America's credibility and moral standing in the world?

ELEANOR CLIFT is a contributing editor for *Newsweek,* a regular panelist on *The McLaughlin Group,* and a political analyst for the Fox News Network. Her latest book is *Founding Sisters and the Nineteenth Amendment,* the story of the seventy-two-year struggle of women to win the right to vote.

Michael
Medved

Thank you for your time, Mr. President. Others may speak to you about sweeping new initiatives that require the mobilization of mass support from the public and your fellow politicians. I want to recommend a simple but shocking change in our government that you can implement immediately with a few strokes of the pen. This dramatic reform can help to take us past the sterile, shopworn liberal-versus-conservative debates and define the nature of your entire presidency.

Mr. President, I urge you unilaterally and instantly to fire at least half of the White House staff. This attention-getting action can set an inspiring example for all dark, cobwebbed corners of the gigantic federal bureaucracy and lead us to a new, nonpartisan determination to make government more efficient and responsible.

It's not that the people who hold these presidential

positions perform poorly in their jobs. It's just that there is no justification for most of these jobs to continue to exist. Far too many human beings enjoy full-time employment at taxpayer expense working directly for the president of the United States, and if you don't believe me, try to get a straight answer from any of your aides as to just how many individuals make up your personal staff. The inability of any of the last three administrations to come up with an honest, consistent answer to that question indicates the nature of the problem. All we know for sure is that more than a thousand people work for you in some aspect of the White House operation, though most insiders will concede that the real number is probably closer to 1,500.

Many years ago, during the Carter administration, I wrote a book called *The Shadow Presidents* that exposed the ridiculous nature of this situation. Looking back at the secret history of America's chief executives and their most important aides, I discovered that this whole idea that a president needs a huge bureaucracy in order to make him look good is a recent aberration. Your predecessor Franklin Roosevelt sustained stunning popularity and won four terms while initiating hundreds of ambitious social programs and leading the most complex, massive series of military campaigns in the history of the human race. He somehow managed to handle these responsibilities despite the fact that his White House staff never exceeded 112—less than one-tenth of the current level!

The duplication of effort involved in the expansion of

the White House staff may have helped to make presidents less powerful, not more so. Consider the growth of the National Security Council and the inevitable tension between the national security adviser and the secretary of state. Getting rid of the separate, redundant "foreign-policy shop" in the White House will only help you avoid all the useless and embarrassing bickering between the National Security Council and the Department of State.

Similarly, you need to eliminate all the White House liaison positions to special-interest groups that currently clutter the executive bureaucracy. Do you really believe that the president needs an array of designated special assistants to help him connect to blacks, Jews, gays, Hispanics, the handicapped, Native Americans, owners of small businesses, and other groups? Wouldn't it make more sense, and prove vastly less patronizing, if you made a point to include members of underrepresented groups as part of your regular, essential staff, rather than ghettoizing them with special assignments relating to their origins?

Everyone acknowledges that government is too big: Bill Clinton, Al Gore, and George W. Bush all promised to trim the wasteful bureaucracy as part of their presidential campaigns. The inability to make the promised cuts represents a failure of will, not an absence of consensus. Now, under the pressure of alarming deficits, liberals and conservatives should develop a joint determination to ruthlessly pare back federal waste and to eliminate some of the two million nonmilitary jobs in our current bloated bureaucracy.

An additional benefit from radical reductions in the size of government—starting with the White House itself—will be a welcome reduction in the shrill, polarizing partisanship that has sickened so many voters in recent years. Let the Democrats show some guts and integrity by standing up to the public employee unions that will thrash and wail over any cuts in useless government jobs; let the Republicans demonstrate similar toughness and idealism by defying the defense contractors and other businesses who will howl and weep over the necessary elimination of corporate welfare. Most citizens will applaud and reward a new spirit of leadership that manages to declare independence from special interests on both sides of the political spectrum.

Immediate, unprecedented cuts in your White House staff will win their own cheers and can begin the process that could inspire and unify public-spirited Americans. I see that my time is up, Mr. President, but your dramatic opportunity is right at hand.

MICHAEL MEDVED hosts a nationally syndicated daily radio talk show focusing on the intersection of politics and pop culture. An honors graduate of Yale, he also studied at Yale Law School, crossing paths with Bill and Hillary Clinton, John Kerry, George W. Bush, and others. His books include *What Really Happened to the Class of '65?, The Shadow Presidents,* and *Hollywood vs. America.*

Catherine
Crier

CATHERINE CRIER, COURT TV ANCHOR AND HOST OF *CATHERINE CRIER LIVE*

Dear Mr. President: We profess to have a republic, a democracy, wherein the people have the right to a transparent government in all but limited, urgent issues of national security. In matters of taxation, real representation, or war, citizens must know the truth. Today, the White House repeatedly presses for corporate tax cuts although most large American businesses pay little or no federal taxes. Thanks to breaks and subsidies, many billion-dollar corporate profiteers receive rebates; taxpayers pay them to earn fortunes in this country. There seems to be no dismay when companies move their mailing addresses to Bermuda. Of course, such action by private citizens would be illegal. The current administration has proposed repealing the corporate alternative minimum tax (AMT) (with rebates from its inception), whereas, increasingly, middle-class voters are captured within its definitions, thereby making their personal tax cuts meaningless.

Most citizens understand that meaningful representation today comes with the size of one's political contributions. Money equals access, and access equals influence. The Republicans have taken the illegal practice of bundling to an entirely new level, as they number, file, and cross-index the names, companies, and industries of your big contributors. We certainly would not want any of those Pioneers or Rangers to fail to get their proper credit or political sway.

Permitting the revolving door between high-level government service and lobbying for corporate America exacerbates this influence. It is unconscionable for individuals to move directly from the halls of Congress or the cabinet to "K Street" to sell their prestige and influence earned at taxpayers' expense. To much fanfare, President Clinton banned this practice by exiting officials for at least five years. He then repealed this order only days before leaving office, to the great relief of his cohorts. Former House Appropriations Committee chair Bob Livingston described it thusly, "I was an advocate for my district and my country. Now I am an advocate for my clients. I don't see a great distinction." I bet most Americans do.

It is equally inappropriate to bring major lobbyists into agency leadership when their prior employment has been so obviously biased as to render their government service a farce. This is currently the case with a dramatic number of your appointments in the EPA, and Departments of the Interior, Agriculture, and Energy, just to name a few. I guess it is more subtle to write legislation as a legitimate job function than to do it on the sly from a lobbyist's office.

No less troublesome are the repeated attempts to shield presidential advisers from appropriate disclosures by asserting executive privilege, whether it be Condoleezza Rice's testimony before the 9/11 Commission or Dick Cheney's list of energy industry leaders he met with allegedly to create national policy. Such information belongs in the public domain.

Finally, the most critical decision that any nation must face is that of whether to send its young men and women to war. The notion of preemptive strikes on another sovereign country is anathema to American principles absent an unambiguous and imminent threat to our homeland. Nothing could be worse than to knowingly whip the public into a frenzy and then lead our young people into battle for a cause not supported by empirical evidence. Such dangerous hypocrisy will surely alienate allies while inviting catastrophic retaliation on our soldiers and civilians alike.

Mr. President, there are many other issues I would like to discuss. However, knowing your time is invaluable, I thank you for this moment.

CATHERINE CRIER, the youngest elected state judge in Texas history, became a television journalist when she left the bench in 1989 to coanchor the evening news for CNN. Crier received an Emmy for her work on ABC's *20/20* and a Dupont-Columbia Award for investigative work on Court TV. Her first book, *The Case Against Lawyers,* was published in 2002 and became a *New York Times* bestseller.

Jane
Seymour

CHARLES BUSH

Mr. President: Given this extraordinary opportunity, I will simply tell you what I would like to see.

I would like to see an end to all religious wars, everywhere. I think it is absurd that in the name of something beautiful and spiritual, we are killing people and teaching children to hate, when the promise of all religion is to love.

In the same spirit, I would like to end all partisan politics. I have spent a lot of time in Washington, and I know that people in government work together to get things done, and yet the political game, as sold to the American people, is one of divisiveness and difference. In reality, government works through the spirit of compromise and negotiation. People should understand that.

I would like to protect the rights of all children. Mr. President, your administration should see to it that a review of our foster-care system is undertaken. We should protect the children in foster care and pave the way for a more effective system of adopting these children.

Lastly, I would like the humanitarian aid that we do sponsor abroad to be much more efficiently delivered. Last year, I was in Africa with the American Red Cross, and I was shocked to see huge sacks of corn stacked at a loading dock, all of it rotten, not one edible piece of corn in the lot. Sure, someone got a tax deduction for sending the surplus corn, and someone got a tax deduction to help finance the delivery program; but no one else benefited. It was so embarrassing it made me want to weep, to see hungry people, standing there in front of heaps of rotten foodstuffs, brought to them with what seemed like supreme indifference.

There are many other burning issues, Mr. President, from the lack of health care in the United States for so many people to literacy problems to the need for more arts in the schools and the assault on a woman's right to choose. These are not only my wishes. They represent the needs of millions of people, in our country and abroad. America can make a difference in these matters, and I appeal to you to use your power to help us do so.

JANE SEYMOUR, a multiple Emmy and Golden Globe winner and a recipient of the Officer of the British Empire (OBE) in the year 2000, has proven her talents in virtually all media: the Broadway stage, motion pictures, and television. Seymour also has successful careers as a designer of homewares and as a painter, exhibiting her artwork in galleries around the world. She serves on the Celebrity Cabinet of the American Red Cross, as an international ambassador for Childhelp USA, and as the honorary chairperson for City Hearts, a Los Angeles–based inner-city youth arts program.

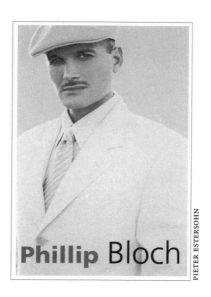

Phillip Bloch

PIETER ESTERSOHN

Dear Mr. President: May I suggest something quite revolutionary: a commissioner of good taste. Yes, I accept. Compassion is always in good taste, Mr. President, never out of style. It goes well with anything, even the red ties, the white shirt, and the blue suit. That Uncle Sam thing you have going on. Mr. President, I think you'll find that while you are being stylish, an icon of good taste, shaking the odd baby and kissing hands or whatever, you can also come into your own as a real person. That's what style can do—bring out the real you, Mr. P. And then you can embark on my special project for you—building a coalition of the real.

Now, my big concerns are the arts, and creating programs for the kids. Our kids are the future; they possess inside themselves all that is to come. Support a federal after-school program; get these kids off the streets whenever possible. You will find that well-funded programs will do that, and the small amount of money invested in them now will save billions later on jails, police, rehabs, court costs, etc. Kids don't really want to do nothing but get in trouble. Give them something to inspire them; the next scientist, doctor, writer, actor, or president is out there waiting to be nurtured and mentored. Good idea, right?

As for you . . . take a walk on the beach sometime, take off these wing tips and ball up the male hose and let your toes squiggle in the sand. Your brain'll kick into gear. You'll get ideas, too. You might even get an insight into how to stop the rising cost of drugs. See, there's another idea!

Now I won't waste my breath going on and on about gay marriage. Let me just say, gays are big influential tax-payers; they have a right to what three-legged people and green people and straight people have. So, please just think of me as one of the good ol' boys and finally give us our equal civil rights.

Where was I? Oh, yeah. I will humbly accept the cabi-net post of czar of good taste. A little chiffon and satin would really brighten this place up and create a prettier place for positive action. My God, it looks like Lincoln slept here! And enough with the bunting. And those long, boring, drab tunnels connecting everything on Capitol Hill (they're a bummer!). Who do I talk to about piping some music in there? A little Beyoncé or Alicia Keys could go a long way. . . . Oh yeah, and since we are being creative, can you legalize weed? Alcohol causes some serious problems, but when people are stoned, they drive five miles per hour and just want to get home and munch out. Just say yes to weed; it's calming, therapeutic and less dangerous, and causes less damage than cigarettes and liquor. The hectic world we live in would become a less stressed place, but for one big mellow traffic jam. Which is better than a war.

Mr. President! However, since we are already in one (it really didn't end in 2003, you know), you must take care of those who are out there fighting to protect us, our glorious country, and our incredible lifestyle. Take care of our soldiers and take care of their families; they have given us so much already. . . . Hey, as the new commissioner of good taste, maybe I would recommend that you hook them up with some kind of makeovers . . . this new coalition is gonna be hot!!! Can't wait to get started. . . .

Keep the faith and keep it real.

PHILLIP BLOCH is an internationally renowned stylist who has dressed some of Hollywood's brightest stars. He is the author of *Elements of Style* and has served as a commentator for CNN and MTV. In addition, Bloch donates his free time to fund-raising for Kelly and Sharon Stone's Planet Hope for Children, the Atlanta Center for the Visually Impaired, and multiple breast cancer and AIDS action/awareness organizations.

Fran Drescher

FIROOZ ZAHEDI

The United States of America, Home of the Brave and Land of the Free, what Thomas Jefferson called "the world's best hope," but I have grave concerns for the future of our country. We seem to be living in a time when the separation between church and state is becoming dangerously blurred. I'm sorry, but there is no place for religion in government. Religion dictates theology, which more often than not justifies violence in the name of righteousness. This is shown in the long history of religious wars leading right up to the present. Mr. President, we must not confuse theology with ideology or we are no better then the enemies we battle overseas.

The opinions of the church must not usurp the principles upon which our country was founded. We are all Americans, created equally and entitled to the same freedoms. Please keep this in mind when government takes a position on same-sex marriages and a woman's right to choose, regardless of what your personal religious beliefs may be. It is your responsibility as an elected official to remain objective when making decisions that affect all the people.

I would also like to address public education. What a shameful place our school system is in! It does not speak well of us as a nation when our children's needs become such a low priority. It is poor judgment and shortsighted to invest only in that which offers an immediate return, and neglect the long-term benefits from educating our young. If you think education is expensive, think how much ignorance costs us. Every American child should be afforded a deluxe education. How else can we ensure our position globally as a powerful nation of forward-thinking individuals?

As for our environment, I beg you to love our planet. Shepherd it as if that is our reason for existing. This magnificent Earth must not be abused for our opportunistic exploitation. We should worship its majestic beauty with devout reverence. I honestly believe there will never be peace from conflict until we live this truth.

And last but not least, I would like to address the unacceptable health-care situation in this country. It is incomprehensible that so many of us live without medical coverage in the richest nation in the world. Why? Perhaps the answer lies in the profit margins of health-insurance companies and their deep-pocketed lobbyists on Capitol Hill. When the "business" of health supersedes the "care" of health, that is capitalism run amok.

There is nothing partisan about sickness, and it is up to Congress to resolve these inequities. Frederick Douglass said, "Power concedes nothing without a demand. It never did and it never will." Our elected officials must hear that the voice of the collective vote is louder and more powerful than the richest insurance lobbyist.

Presidents come and go but the strength and integrity of our Constitution is what prevails. Mr. President, be a benevolent leader who realizes that this nation is not made up of nuts and bolts in a large corporate machine but rather of people with needs.

FRAN DRESCHER was nominated twice for both Golden Globe and Emmy awards for her performance in the CBS series *The Nanny*. She is also a writer, director, executive producer, and two-time *New York Times* bestselling author. Drescher is an activist and advocate for improved health care, better education, and a cleaner environment.

John Paul
DeJoria

If I had five private minutes with the next president of the United States, I would say, first off, "Mr. President, this'll only take a minute." And then—and this would apply no matter which party he was from, because it's the nature of the game: "Mr. President, I know you owe a great deal in political favors to those who helped get you here. But now you are here. And though I don't want to tell you how to play the game, I will ask that you be careful most of all not to hurt the people of the United States, or threaten the environment, or deal unfairly with the business community as you pay off those debts. Try to be a president for all the people. If you mess up, admit that you are human, like the rest of us, and then try to correct the mistake. Our nation will love it.

"We are still a government 'of the people, for the people, and by the people.' We are the people that you represent. Don't overtax us. Be fair and establish a flat tax so no one will complain.

"I wish you my best and will probably support you no matter what, because you are president."

JOHN PAUL DEJORIA is an actor and successful businessman. In addition to his contributions to The Creative Coalition, DeJoria gives time and money to the Rainforest Foundation, the American Paralysis Association, St. Jude Children's Hospital, the AIDS Relief Fund for beauty professionals, and other charitable organizations.

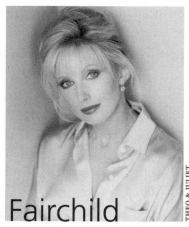

Morgan Fairchild

THEO & JULIET

Dear Mr. President: I know you are a man of good intentions, but good intentions are not enough for the leader of the free world. They are not enough to justify the invasion of another country. And good intentions may be the only rationale left, now that all the originally offered reasons have been proven to be false.

I doubt that you see the good intentions that motivated many of us who opposed the war. It is not that we don't love our country or our men and women in uniform. It is that we don't like to see them misused, whatever the intentions.

I fully supported attacking Al Qaeda in Afghanistan in response to 9/11—I only wished that we could have truthfully said "mission accomplished" before we tried to start the next. Many other countries felt the same way. However, rather than building an international coalition, we chose to act almost alone in the expectation that weapons of mass destruction would be found and our actions judged correct. This turned out to be a dream.

Many of us did not question whether Iraq possessed WMDs but rather whether an invasion was wise at that time and in that manner. There were many people with long years of experience in the Middle East who warned that if we went in, we would be likely to end up exactly where we are now. To think otherwise would be to be dreaming.

Few thought Saddam Hussein was a good man or a good leader, but unfortunately, the world abounds with bad men and bad leaders. We could never hope to depose all of them. And even if we were to set out to do just that, how could we be sure that those who would replace the tyrants would be better men or better leaders? Our president no doubt had good intentions when he offered democracy as a gift to the Iraqis. Thinking they would value this more than electricity or jobs was a naive dream.

Mr. President, the road to hell is paved with good intentions. And some dreams are nightmares.

MORGAN FAIRCHILD was propelled to stardom in 1981 when she landed the role of Constance Carlyle in *Flamingo Road,* for which she was nominated for a Golden Globe for best actress. She also starred in the television series *Falcon Crest* and *Paper Dolls.* During its ten-year run, Fairchild played Chandler Bing's mom on *Friends.* She is a member of the Entertainment Industry AIDS Task Force and an active speaker on environmental issues of all kinds, and helped found the Environmental Communications Office, which encourages entertainment-industry professionals to become better educated and more active on environmental issues.

Tony
Goldwyn

Mr. President: I have no quarrel with your party or with your obvious loyalty to an organization that has shown you such devotion over the years. I have no desire to impugn your patriotism or your fervent belief that we live in the greatest nation on Earth.

What I do take exception to, and what causes me grave concern, is your propensity to filter all issues, every decision that crosses your desk, through the lens of party politics and electioneering. Furthermore, I see a dangerously increasing trend in the White House of catering to very powerful and very rich special interests whose agenda and ideology are on the fringes of mainstream thought.

We live in a time when the media has attached itself to extremists: be they suicide bombers or bombers of abortion clinics. The press is drawn to the outrageous, the shocking, the unfathomable like moths to a flame. Just take a look at reality TV: *Fear Factor, Survivor, Who Wants to Be a Millionaire?* Those on the fringe may be the minority, but they are making the most noise.

Our media-driven culture has also latched onto the sound bite as the great communication device. Hence, all issues tend to be boiled down to their simplest, most digestible form. Black and white, bottom line, good versus bad, us versus them, rule our decision-making process. That dreaded gray area, where questions have more than one answer and require real introspection and creative thought, has been painted over in favor of the bold tones of absolutism and certainty. We're right, they're wrong, and that's it!

As the chief executive of this country, you have the power to set the tone of our national debate. You are the living symbol of America. When you speak you speak for each and every one of us.

In fulfilling that sacred duty, I implore you not to allow the fringes to frame the debate on any issue. I ask you to listen deeply to your opposition on all matters, to internalize the concerns of the person on the opposite side of the table, whether he is a member of the opposition party or an adversary in war, a fundamentalist cleric in Iraq or a jobless worker at home.

America remains a beacon of hope and freedom in the world. By definition, we are a people open to all points of view, inclusive of all ideologies. As president, you embody that ideal. By truly empathizing with your opposition even as you forcefully communicate your own perspective,

you have the opportunity to forge a collective consciousness among our people that will write a national agenda
in a truly representative way.

So, Mr. President, as our national communicator, help
us to embrace and understand complexity rather than be
afraid of it. Help us to listen to and consider those whose
views are unfathomable to us, and in so doing, help us
forge lasting solutions to deeply intricate national and
global problems. This is the essence of leadership. It is the
essence of the American spirit.

TONY GOLDWYN, actor and director, serves as copresident of The Creative Coalition. His numerous credits
include leading roles in *The Last Samurai, The Pelican
Brief,* and *Ghost,* as well as directing the film *A Walk on
the Moon.*

Barry
Bostwick

For me, what would be most telling in a "one-on-one" session with the president wouldn't be his views on policies, but rather what he might reveal about the essence of his personality. We all know that even the most brilliant, innovative minds can get things accomplished only if they effectively communicate what they want to those who can then successfully execute the plan. In short, it takes leadership, built out of attitude, personality, and ease with others without giving away any personal agenda—don't let them see the wheels turning, so to speak. "Compassionate" persuasion is the key. I would want to have a conversation that might show me what he was made of, how he related to people, what mattered to him. I don't think it's so important to look at political failures and successes; it would be hard for me to assess the man's character purely through his political record anyway. I would be reassured enough on that score simply to know that he's still in the game and that he's learned from his experience. You expect a politician to know his politics, and know how to play them. But, as for the elders of any tribe, "wisdom" is the key and deciding factor, wisdom about everyday life. How do you recognize a wise man? How can you measure a person's knowledge, insight, and judgment? If I had my chance, I'd ask about kids, hobbies, and ex-wives!

BARRY BOSTWICK is an award-winning actor who has earned critical acclaim for his work on stage, screen, and television. After six years playing the mayor on ABC's *Spin City,* he has continued to work in all mediums. Outspoken about his bout with prostate cancer, Bostwick was presented with the Courage Award by President Clinton.

Daniel  Stern

SOPHIE STERN

If I had five minutes with the next president, I would say, "John, your top two priorities are going to be protecting our country and healing our country."

The lack of spending for domestic security, especially when compared to the costs of the blundering war in Iraq, is unconscionable. For our tax dollar, Americans' minimum expectation is that we are pooling our resources for at least one common cause, domestic security. Take some of that rebuilding money, or some of that fat-cat tax cut and get every piece of security equipment on the market. Fund X-raying cargo, airport screeners, border patrol, and first responders. Let's get control of this country. Let's know who and what is coming in and out. Who knows, it might even help in the last unwinnable war we waged before the War on Terror, the long-forgotten War on Drugs, as well as force us to deal with our pressing illegal-immigration problems. And let's get the FBI and the CIA new computers because evidently they are still using Atari computers. They probably like to relax by playing Pong. Yes, let's go after Al Qaeda and bin Laden. Let's root out terrorists when we find them. (Let's also address the root causes of the anti-Americanism that was behind 9/11 and that has now been inflamed by an ill-conceived and corrupt war.) But mostly, as an American, I want to protect America and its citizens. Let's definitely not do this on the cheap.

Healing, however, may be more difficult. Sometimes it feels like our country is on the verge of civil war. The war that Newt Gingrich and his right-wing cronies declared on Democrats has continued to fray the fabric that holds this country together—the validity of our government. Impeaching a president for a sexual transgression, the insistence in not counting all the votes in Florida, and now the entire, right-wing agenda of your predecessor enraged Democrats to a breaking point. And Republicans, after so many years of being in the minority, are holding on to Bush's coattails as tight as they can. So, Mr. President, you have your work cut out for you. There is a lot to undo—the mess in Iraq, our diminished reputation in the world's eyes, children left behind, the environment, as well as the financial deficit are all going to have to be addressed. But your biggest challenge is to get the people of this country moving in the same direction again.

With my last two minutes, I'd like to offer some solutions. Build a bipartisan cabinet. And introduce a Clean

Government Plan that would address not only campaign finance reform but standards for congressional-district line drawing, voting machines, etc. Give this country a common cause. We can come together to accomplish the most amazing things when they are good and right. We've been to the moon, we won World War II, and we survived 9/11. Implementing a Mission for Energy Independence would galvanize the country, create jobs, clean the environment, and free us from dependence on shady characters for our life's blood.

DANIEL STERN has appeared in numerous movies, including *Diner, Home Alone, Hannah and Her Sisters,* and *Breaking Away.* He was the narrator of the hit TV show *The Wonder Years* and has done extensive work in the theater both in New York and Los Angeles, most recently in *Dinner with Friends* at the Geffen Playhouse. He directed the fantasy baseball movie *Rookie of the Year* and made his debut as a playwright when his play *Barbra's Wedding* premiered in New York in February 2003.

Hector
Elizondo

AUDIE ENGLAND

Dear Mr. President: First, I wish to acknowledge my appreciation regarding the enormity of your task during these troubled times. Challenge brings out the best or worst in us. Crisis has now given us an opportunity to invigorate a rebirth of what for many of us is the great American experiment, a beacon of democratic ideals. The great republic reflecting progressive, innovative, all-inclusive, humanistic values. The champion of the just and not just the champion.

I husband an indelible image that keeps me anchored to my American dream; the great Lincoln pacing the floors of the White House, enduring another sleepless night, shrouded in doubt and apprehension, wrestling with the choices and the ultimate consequences of his and his administration's decisions. He, like you and I, had faith, but it was doubt and not oversimplified certainty that led to his education. That doubt can only be creative if it leads to dialogue and healthy debate. The path is never clear when it is shrouded in secrecy. Obscurity is not the friend of democracy.

I therefore beseech you to encourage the news media (which is, unfortunately, more often than not, in the business of entertainment) to ask the uncomfortable questions, to dig deep, to doubt and ultimately clarify, because that is their job. They must not be a tool of any administration. It only makes us weaker, not stronger. Our republic's future depends on informed citizens with the ability to indulge in hard, nuanced analysis, not dangerous and misleading jingoism. That path only makes us seem small and arrogant. We need friends on this endangered planet, Mr. President.

In medieval times it was the court jester's job to speak truth to power and say what no one dared to say. Beware of men of messianic fervor. They will not tell you the truth. They will throw the dart, then paint the target. The devil can also quote Scripture.

Pace the floors, Mr. President, let your shadow flicker on the walls of the White House, burning the midnight oil. We need you. Godspeed.

HECTOR ELIZONDO is an award-winning star of screen and stage. His movie credits include *Raising Helen, The Princess Diaries I* and *II, Runaway Bride,* and *Pretty Woman.* His early career was marked by a stage success in *Steambath,* for which he won an Obie. Elizondo is a member of The Creative Coalition's board of directors.

Lawrence Bender

Mr. President, I feel that this country is at a critical juncture in its history. I never thought I would hear the terms *Vietnam* and *quagmire* used to refer to anything other than what America endured in the 1960s, but I have heard them tossed around a lot lately to describe the current state of affairs in Iraq.

And I believe the war in Iraq has the potential to have a far more devastating impact on world stability than our presence in Southeast Asia ever did. But it is not too late to change the troubling direction we are heading in. A great opportunity was squandered in the wake of 9/11, when a considerable part of the world said they were one with us. We could have joined with them as an international force for good, but we didn't . . . yet it is not too late. It will take an extraordinary kind of leadership to do so now, and I believe you have it in yourself to provide just that.

Mr. President, I ask you to use the bully pulpit your position affords you to inspire and convince all Americans that if we are to help reshape our world, we must first reshape our own society. The priority should not be on our own narrow self-interests but on how each of us can contribute to the restoration of our sense of collective purpose. It's not about shopping our troubles away; it's about each of us sacrificing for the greater good. And we have to start seriously addressing the causes of our vulnerability rather than ignoring them.

A practical thing you could do, Mr. President, is to work to lessen our dependence on foreign oil. I know that the energy industries are very close to the levers of power and always have been, but it is essential that our judgment in the Middle East not be clouded by our enormous dependency on what is under the ground there. Incentives for finding alternative means of power would provide us with a more solid ground from which to broker a lasting peace in that region. It would give us more credibility with our allies as well. We have a technology today, the hybrid car, that should be supported as one of the means by which to wean ourselves off of foreign oil.

Let's invest in building new energy technologies, and developing new, homegrown industries that show the way for the rest of the world. We have spent an enormous amount of capital—both political and financial—to buy friends in the Middle East. We give $20 billion a year to Saudi Arabia alone. For every friend this money buys, it also buys an enemy. As you know, fifteen of the nineteen 9/11 hijackers came from that country.

Mr. President, at this most volatile and dangerous moment, we need visionary leadership, brave and bold, like back in the days of JFK, when he said that we were going to put a man on the moon by the end of the decade. No one took a poll. He said, this is my vision. And we did it. That was real leadership—the kind we need again today. We need to take another giant step for America, and for mankind.

LAWRENCE BENDER, a producer, has had his films honored with nineteen Academy Award nominations, including two for best picture. A longtime collaborator of Quentin Tarantino's, Bender also serves on the board of The Creative Coalition, the Israel Policy Forum, and Rock the Vote, and is a member of the Natural Resources Defense Council Executive Forum.

FRAZER PENNEBAKER

Sam
Moore

Dear Mr. President: I realize you truly have your hands full, given the monumental changes in how the world is turning because of the end of the Cold War and the advent of the age of terrorism, zealots, crazies, and misguided megalomaniacs with access to nuclear arms, but I've been asked to speak to you, given an opportunity to make a dent somewhere for someone, so I've decided to ask you for some help to resolve an issue that's been around but never properly addressed since October of 1961 and that, in comparison, seems relatively calm and sane.

There are so many issues that affect the recording artist community that are all terribly important because many impact our health and pension rights and benefits and our livelihoods. They are too complicated to deal with in this short essay, so I offer a narrow but grand issue that could truly use your help.

Most people are under the impression that when they hear their favorite song on the radio or at a restaurant, in a stadium, or in an elevator, the artist whose performance they are enjoying receives some compensation. Surprise! The only parties being compensated for that broadcast are the publisher and the writer(s) of the song, not the artist, who gets absolutely nothing.

Because in our great country the recording artists get no recompense for the broadcasting of their performances on the radio, in those elevators, and anywhere else, they are shut out and have little or no hope to retrieve the payments. For their performances in all the other countries of the world, however, this right to a payment for broadcast performances is guaranteed by an International Treaty called the Rome Convention. The Rome Convention is not a complicated document, but what it asks the broadcasters to do was considered out of the question in the richest, most fertile media market in the world. It would have required the broadcasters and other end users to pay some pennies into a separate fund that would govern performance rights for the artists.

The issue has been to Capitol Hill a few times in the past forty years. Senator Orrin Hatch has from time to time fought a good fight to do the right thing. Still, those who oppose participating in it have huge dollars and even greater power because, for the most part, they own and control our airwaves. This independence of ownership of the airwaves in the United States is the basic reason our artists, who have given us all so much listening pleasure for all of these decades, receive nada.

It is estimated that this system would cost stations only about $12,000 a year, based on a $.07 per play per song. But what that $1,000 per month per station would mean to the recording artists is thousands and thousands of dollars even at pennies per play because it becomes global, and I would bet that even my song "Soul Man" is played several hundred times a day around the world. At $.03 or $.04 a pop, I have been projected to earn well over $50,000 a year globally. That earning would mean I wouldn't, at sixty-eight years old, have to run up and down the road. I would qualify for all of my health benefits, be a burden to no one, and enjoy singing and performing just like guys who made way more hits and had way more success than even my gold and platinum hits, my Grammy Awards, and my induction into the Rock and Roll Hall of Fame.

Now I was only using myself as an example. There are many of my peers and their families whose lives would be enriched so that they could afford to keep the kids and the grandkids in school, eat well, sleep well, and finally have some of the fruits of their labor

So, Mr. President, I ask you to help us rectify one of the many wrongs that fall on the recording artist group and see if we could finally see some light at the end of a tunnel that isn't coming from an oncoming train.

SAM MOORE is a Grammy-winning member of the Rock and Roll Hall of Fame; he has also been dubbed the "Frank Sinatra of Soul" by B. B. King and was recently introduced by Bruce Springsteen as the "greatest living soul singer on planet Earth."

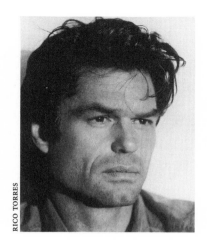

RICO TORRES

Harry
Hamlin

My name is Buford Collins and I'm the luckiest guy in the world. You've probably heard my story by now. I've been on Jay Leno and even Letterman, and I've met that pretty Katie girl who's on in the morning. I've even met the president! In the Oval Office! All because they say I'm one of the last great shoe shiners in America. Yep, I've been shining folks' shoes at Grand Central for almost sixty years, so someone said I should be famous and now I am. They say I'm good at my job because I can bring up a fine shine on just about any shoe ever made and because I like to engage my clients in what they call "challenging conversation." Now, I'm not sure exactly what that means. I never had much schooling and I don't take much to reading and writing and such, but I do keep my eyes and ears open, and golly, I've heard a few things and seen a few things in my day. Now, it takes about five minutes to bring up a shine on a pair of wing tips and you'd be surprised how much can be said in five minutes. Take, for example, the time I was invited to shine the president's shoes. Imagine me, Buford P. Collins, from Trenton, New Jersey, in the White House! Well, they took me into this big white room with plates on the wall and there he was. He wasn't as tall as I'd pictured him, and when he shook my hand, I could smell his breath. It smelled like he'd had maybe a Caesar salad for lunch. I asked if I could shine his shoes and he said he'd be honored. I put my box down on the floor and he sat down in what looked like a chair made of pure silk in front of the fireplace. He had on a fine pair of Italian cordovan wing tips, and when he pulled up his cuffs, I noticed that, like most men, he didn't put any moisturizer on his shins in the morning. I almost told him he ought to but thought better of it. Then, as I started to apply the first conditioning coat, he said, "Buford, I consider a man who does what you do to be a man smack-dab in the middle of it all. What's your take on how things are going?" Well, I'd already decided not to do much talking, but he just opened the door, so I said to myself, "What the hell?" I asked the president if he minded if I spit-shined. He looked at me kinda funny; almost like maybe he should ask the Secret Service and then said it'd be okay. I spat as nicely as I could on his right shoe and started to answer his question. I said I was just an old guy who shines people's shoes but that I'd seen an awful lot of comings and goings down at the station and that I'd talked to a lot of folks over the years. I said that it seemed to me that

America had changed. I said I remembered when I was proud to be part of something that everyone knew was really good, sort of like being part of a winning football team that did a lot of charity work in the off-season. I said that I didn't feel that way anymore and I told him why. I said that for one thing, we'd lost our self-respect, and that as far as I could tell, you won't get anyone else's respect if you don't respect yourself. I said that I thought that respect comes from the choices we make every day and the intentions behind those choices. I said that a country as big and strong as ours ought to have the respect of the rest of the world, especially after what we did to help out the world during the last big world war and even more especially after what happened on September 11. I said I wondered how, after those things, we could have lost so much respect around the world. I said I thought that maybe we'd become too big for our britches. The president started fidgeting with his feet and I told him to hold still. I spat on the other shoe and said that we got punched in the eye with 9/11 but that that didn't mean we were allowed to start punching everyone else. I said that we ought to be leaders in the world. He pulled his shoe out from under my cloth and said that we were the greatest superpower in the world and that we were the biggest leader. I pulled his shoe back and said, "You have to hold still, Mr. President." Then I said that everyone watches us because we are so big and that they do what we do, just like kids do what their parents do, not what they say. I said that we needed to look at all the problems in the world, like hunger, and global climate change, and the problems of people who feel they are being exploited or oppressed, and how to find cleaner energy sources, and that we needed to try to find long-term solutions to those things in a really honest way and in a way that shows that we really care. Because that's how you get respect; you show people that you care about them and their problems. I said the terrorism thing was a pretty tough problem but that it probably couldn't be fixed by killing or capturing all the terrorists because every time you kill one, another two will pick up a gun like that monster that Hercules had to kill that kept growing new heads every time he cut one off. I said that there wouldn't be enough jails or gravediggers if that's how we went about getting rid of terrorism. Now the president tried to stand up but I said, "You asked me Mr. President, so I'm telling you. Now sit down. I still have to put on the final shine." He sighed like a kid being scolded by his mom and sat back down. I said that, sure, you had to go after the bad guys but that you also had to have empathy for the young Muslim kids out there who feel like they are being wronged by us. If they didn't feel that way, they wouldn't join up with the terrorists and go around killing people. I said that if he was smart, he'd try to figure out why they're so mad and try to fix that. Killing them is just going to make 'em madder. The president shouted, "That would be giving in to them. . . . Capitulation!!" He seemed mad himself now. I said that I didn't know what *capitulation* meant but that if he just kept getting a bigger stick to kill them, he'd better order a lot more body bags for us. He stood up as I was doing what I call the final power shine. It takes lots of elbow grease. I said I was almost done, and that I really only had one more thing to say, so he sat back down, sighing louder this time. I said that if he just really cared about the world and all the people in it and not just about the people that helped him get into the White House, then we'd have our self-respect back and most likely the respect of the world and then we'd do things like find a new, clean energy source and stop global warming and find ways to feed everyone and help the Palestinians and Israelis find a solution and balance the budget and improve our health care and save Social Security and reduce the trade deficit and really help the Iraqis find themselves. Because if the world believes that we really care about it, it will stop fearing us and help us do the right thing. I had worked up quite a sweat doing the final power shine but it seemed to help me get that last bit out. As the president stood, he frowned at me for a split second then smiled a big smile and I could see that his teeth were in pretty good shape for a man his age. I put my kit together, and when I stood up, the president put his hand on my shoulder and sort of pointed me toward the door. As we paced across the room he said, "Bud . . . you mind if I call you Bud?" I thought for a moment that he had forgotten my name and then I remembered that he liked nicknames. I said, "You can call me what you like, Mr. President." When we got to the door, he put his arm all the way around my shoulders and turned me to face a photographer who was wearing a bow tie. He said, "Cheese!" and the camera flashed. Then he said, "Bud, I'll think about what you said, and that was just about one of the best shoe shines I ever had. Thanks." And with that I was out the door. On the train that night I wondered if the president really liked the shine. He had said as much . . . or had he? "Just about one of the best shoe shines I ever had." It sounded good but I guessed that that could also mean "not quite" one of the best, but I was too tired to think about it anymore and I fell asleep.

HARRY HAMLIN is an actor and environmentalist whose main focus is the development of clean alternative energy sources. He is currently helping shepherd a new technology called Plasma Energy Generation in conjunction with the University of California at Irvine. Best known for his role as attorney Michael Kuzak on NBC's *L.A. Law,* Hamlin has also appeared in *Clash of the Titans, Making Love,* TV's *Studs Lonnigan,* and the sitcom *Movie Stars.*

About
The Creative Coalition

The Creative Coalition is a nonprofit, nonpartisan 501(c)(3) association comprised of concerned, committed professionals from the arts and entertainment communities. It was founded in 1989 by Ron Silver, Christopher Reeve, Susan Sarandon, Stephen Collins, and others to educate members on, and stimulate constructive dialogue about, vital public issues.

Every American citizen has a right—and a duty—to participate in the political process. All of us, no matter our profession or point of view, have an obligation to contribute to the national dialogue about the myriad issues that confront our nation and our communities. This fundamental principle of citizenship applies to everyone, regardless of who they are, what they do, or where they live.

As members of the arts and entertainment community, many of us believe that our obligations as citizens are particularly strong. Because of our role in shaping American culture—and because of our visibility—political activity and issue advocacy take on special meaning for we actors, directors, writers, artists, executives, and others who work in the creative professions. The Creative Coalition was created by us and for us to ensure that our involvement in the political and policy-making process is well informed and constructively channeled.

Many of us, after all, are adept communicators, skilled in the art of persuasion. Many Coalition members are also highly visible public figures whose celebrity ensures a strong voice—a voice we may use to direct public attention to the issues about which we care deeply.

We play a privileged role in national life. Throughout American history, artists, writers, and entertainers have addressed political issues through their work. In our free society, novels, movies, music, and all the arts have often had a profound impact on political discourse. But today many within the creative world speak out, directly and forcefully, not just through their work, but also as citizens and individuals.

The Creative Coalition exists to educate, organize, and mobilize the arts and entertainment communities to ensure that those voices are strong, clear, focused, and knowledgeable.

Today, the Coalition is made up of hundreds of actors, writers, directors, producers, journalists, artists, agents, casting directors, attorneys, publicists, dancers, artists, singers, and anyone within the creative professions who takes his or her role as a citizen seriously. Coalition members are caring, concerned professionals who believe that the active involvement in our political system of this highly visible industry is important not just to those who participate, but to the nation as a whole.

The Creative Coalition believes that those of us who help create American culture have an obligation to be involved in the political process that governs it. We are eager to explore the issues and ideas that are at the forefront of national discourse. And we are willing to seek a greater understanding of those issues before we seek to affect them.

The Coalition's programs, initiatives, and events serve two functions: issue education for both the public and the entertainment industry, and direct advocacy on national issues of vital importance. As successful creative professionals, we have been given a voice . . . and The Creative Coalition helps us use it powerfully and effectively.

Members participate in invitation-only forums, seminars, and briefings aimed at strengthening our voice on national issues. The Creative Coalition staff also helps individual members research issues of personal importance and help frame arguments that can be used effectively in public appearances and presentations.

We mobilize the skills and resources of the actors, writers, producers, designers, musicians, executives, and others whose place within society offers them a unique opportunity to affect the political process and public policy. By joining or supporting this potent coalition of your colleagues and friends, you can strengthen your voice as a citizen and advocate, and in so doing serve not just your art, but the nation as a whole.

Tony Goldwyn and Joe Pantoliano (Copresidents)

The Creative Coaliton
665 Broadway
New York, New York 10012
www.thecreativecoalition.org

AUG 2 0 2004